Contents

Sharks

All sharks are carnivores, and many are potentially dangerous to man. They are unpredictable, but certain precautions can minimize a possible attack. Do not swim or dive alone. Stay out of the water if sharks are in the area. Don't swim when bleeding, and boat all fish immediately. Do not provoke, molest or spear any shark, no matter how small. Of the more than 200 species of sharks, sizes range from a ten-inch dogfish to the largest of all fishes, the 45-foot whale shark. Sharks have a skeletal structure made up entirely of cartilage.

1 **Tiger shark** *(Galeocerdo cuvieri)* This is the largest and most notorious member of the requiem shark family. The vertical bars on its sides (which fade somewhat with age) and the broad, blunt snout contribute to the ferocity of its appearance. The tiger rarely grows longer than 16 feet, but it is reputed to exceed 20 feet. Powerful jaws along with serrate teeth are capable of cutting pieces from carapaces of large sea turtles.

2 **Great hammerhead** *(Sphyrna mokarran)* For no proven function, the eyes and nostrils of all hammerhead sharks are located at the tips of the lateral lobes on the head, making them the most recognizable of all sharks. The great hammerhead, a voracious feeder, may exceed 20 feet.

Commensals

Commensals, meaning those that eat at the same table, is the term describing several species of fish commonly seen accompanying sharks and other large fish. It is believed they benefit by sharing scattered morsels of food when the host fish feeds. Sharksuckers and remoras attach themselves by means of a suction disk on top of their heads. Pilotfish, rudderfish and cobia swim freely.

3 **Pilotfish** *(Naucrates ductor)* is a two-foot-long member of the jack family.

4 **Banded rudderfish** *(Seriola zonata)* is another jack. When it attains one foot or longer, it loses its bars and no longer accompanies sharks.

5 **Sharksucker** *(Echeneis naucrates)* is a large member of the remora family, growing to over three feet.

6 **Remora** *(Remora remora)* is the most common species of its genus.

7 **Cobia** *(Rachycentron canadum)* mimic the sharksucker in appearance and behavior when less than three feet long. As they mature, reaching to over five feet, they become more solitary and rarely accompany sharks.

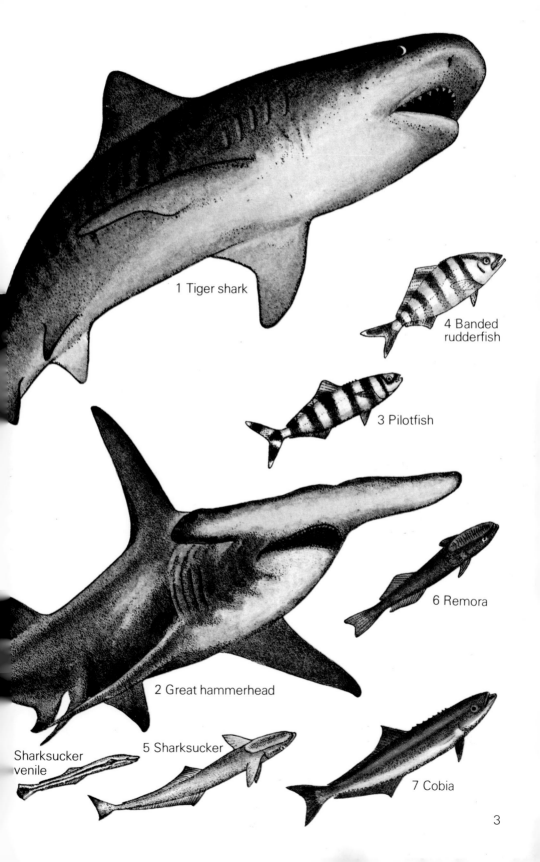

1 Tiger shark

4 Banded rudderfish

3 Pilotfish

2 Great hammerhead

6 Remora

Sharksucker venile

5 Sharksucker

7 Cobia

3

1 **Bull shark** *(Carcharhinus leucas)*
A potential danger to swimmers, the
bull shark frequents inshore waters
and sometimes enters rivers. A broadly-
rounded snout and heavy, compact body
distinguish this shark. The bull
shark may grow to ten feet.

2 **Lemon Shark** *(Negaprion brevirostris)*
This slim-bodied shark has a second
dorsal fin almost as large as the first.
The lemon is found in the same inshore
waters as the bull shark, though they
do not travel together. Like most
sharks, its color varies, but the lemon
is usually a shade of yellowish brown.
Length is up to 11 feet.

3 **Nurse shark** *(Ginglymostoma cirratum)*
This shark grows to 14 feet, and has
a distinctive tail lacking an extended
lower lobe. It is the only Atlantic
shark with barbels. Found most often in
shallow water, it may lie motionless
on the bottom.

4 **Blacktip shark** *(Carcharhinus limbatus)*
A long-snouted coastal shark, the
blacktip is aptly named for the dark
markings tipping some of its fins.
This fast-swimming shark is often seen
jumping from the water.

5 **Sand tiger** *(Odontaspis taurus)*
The young and some adults of this
species are marked with irregular
spots or blotches. They have two
equal-sized dorsal fins and reach
a maximum length of nine feet.

Sharks

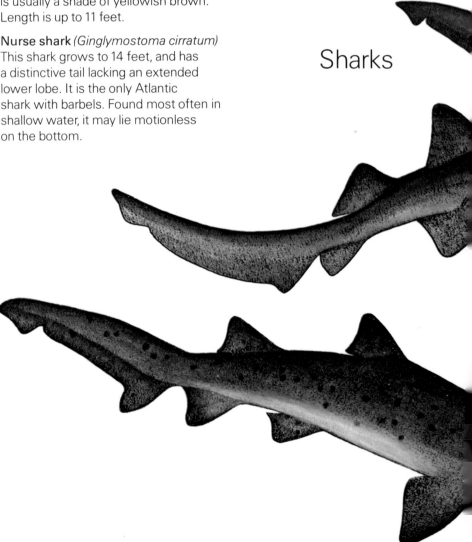

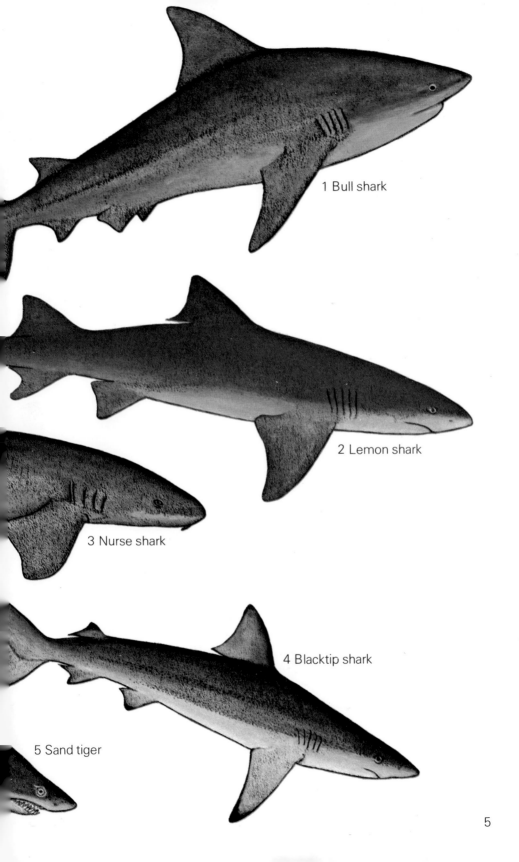

1 Bull shark

2 Lemon shark

3 Nurse shark

4 Blacktip shark

5 Sand tiger

Rays

Rays vary in form from an almost
perfect diamond shape to a disk.
Though often seen lying motionless on
the bottom partly buried in sand, they are strong
swimmers propelled by graceful undulations of their
winglike pectoral fins. The mouth and gill slits are on the
underside of the body, with the eyes on the upper side.
A pair of large openings behind the eyes enables most rays
to draw in water for breathing without having to open
the mouth. Stingrays have a serrated spine on the upper
surface of the tail base, which may be venomous. A stab
from this spine can cause extreme pain; however, unless
stepped on or otherwise molested, rays are harmless.

2 Southern stingray

1 **Spotted eagle ray** *(Aetobatus narinari)*
This large ray (up to eight feet
long) has a well-defined head set
off from its pectoral fins. Like
the manta, this is an active ray.

2 **Southern stingray** *(Dasyatis americana)*
The winglike pectoral fins of this ray
extend forward to encompass the head.
A pale spot before the eyes marks
the five-foot-wide disk.

3 **Atlantic manta** *(Manta birostris)*
Mantas grow to a monstrous size of
over 20 feet and 3000 pounds. Also
called devilfish, they pose little
threat to man. Unlike other rays, the
mouth is in front. Limblike flaps
project from the head forward of the
eyes. Mantas swim with mouths open,
straining food from the water.

4 **Smalltooth sawfish** *(Pristis pectinata)*
Sweeping through schools of small fish,
this sharklike ray feeds by slashing
with its tooth-edged saw. The
smalltooth sawfish reaches 20 feet.

5 **Yellow stingray** *(Urolophus jamaicensis*
Though small, with a mottled disk no
wider than 15 inches, the yellow
stingray can inflict pain from its spine
if stepped on or carelessly handled.

3 Atlantic manta

4 Smalltooth sawfish

5 Yellow stingray

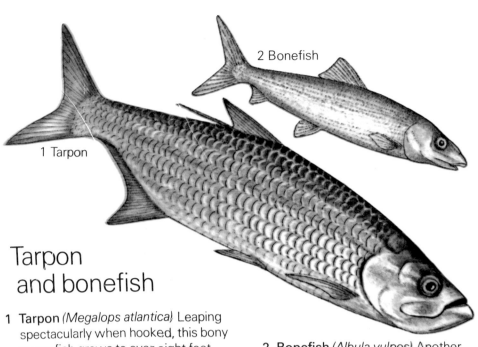

1 Tarpon

2 Bonefish

Tarpon and bonefish

1 **Tarpon** *(Megalops atlantica)* Leaping spectacularly when hooked, this bony game fish grows to over eight feet. Large silvery scales and a bright-hued stripe along the dorsal area distinguish the tarpon.

2 **Bonefish** *(Albula vulpes)* Another superb game fish, bonefish inhabit salt and brackish water shallows. Length is up to three feet.

Morays

As beautiful and repulsive as the snakes they resemble, these fish have smooth, scaleless skin. Narrow, muscular jaws can drive the fanglike teeth deeply into anything they grasp. The bite itself is not toxic, but since the teeth invariably are contaminated with decayed food particles, serious infection may follow if the wound is not treated. Largely nocturnal and secretive by nature, morays hide in crevices and under coral ledges. They are generally harmless to man unless provoked. Morays should never be eaten, since some individuals of all species are capable of causing severe food poisoning, or even death.

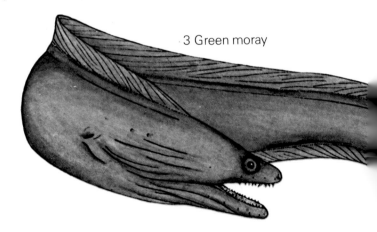

3 Green moray

Green moray *(Gymnothorax funebris)*
This species reaches the greatest size of
Atlantic morays, more than six feet. The
green color is the result of a yellowish
mucus overlaying the dark blue skin.

Goldentail moray *(Muraena miliaris)*
A small moray not exceeding two feet,
the goldentail moray has tiny teeth
even for its size. The attractive
yellow markings vary greatly, but
the golden color is most extensive and
pronounced at the tail tip.

Spotted moray *(Gymnothorax moringa)*
This moray is usually found in shallow
water coral and rock areas. It may grow
to four feet.

6 Viper moray *(Enchelycore nigricans)*
Strongly arched jaws expose the many
awesome teeth of the viper moray even
when the mouth is closed. This eel
ranges up to three feet long.

7 Purplemouth moray *(Gymnothorax
vicinus)* Varying in body color from
a nearly uniform brown to a densely-
mottled pattern, the purplemouth
may grow to four feet. The dark
purplish color inside the lower jaw
contrasts with pale lavender at the roof.

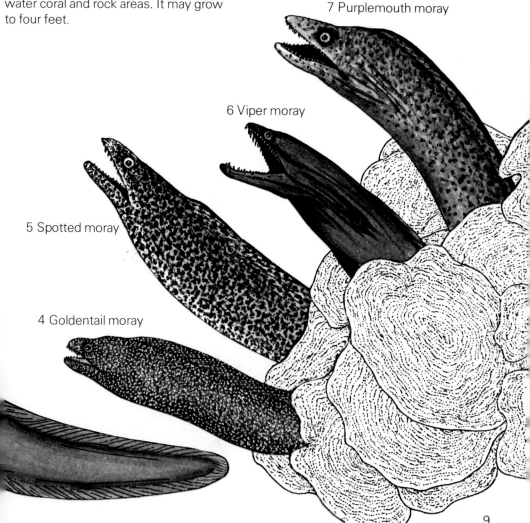

7 Purplemouth moray

6 Viper moray

5 Spotted moray

4 Goldentail moray

Barracudas

1 **Southern sennet** *(Sphyraena picudilla)* This barracuda, which grows to 18 inches, is harmless and good to eat.

2 **Great barracuda** *(Sphyraena barracuda)* Though guilty of some attacks on humans in poor visibility situations or when speared, the great barracuda poses a more serious threat to man when eaten than from an attack. It has probably caused more fish poisoning than any other fish. These fierce predators may grow to six feet, but are seldom more than four feet long.

Snook

3 **Snook** *(Centropomus undecimalis)* An extremely popular food and game fish, snook may grow to over four feet.

Slim-bodied fishes

4 **Sand diver** *(Synodus intermedius)* This cigar-shaped lizardfish may burrow in sand if disturbed, leaving only its eyes exposed. A sand diver can reach 18 inches

5 **Trumpetfish** *(Aulostomus maculatus)* Often seen standing on its head to mimic part of the seascape, this fish has a single barbel on its chin. Though it appears lethargic, its long snout acts like a suction tube, so that small fish and shrimp seem to vanish into its mouth Trumpetfish can grow to three feet.

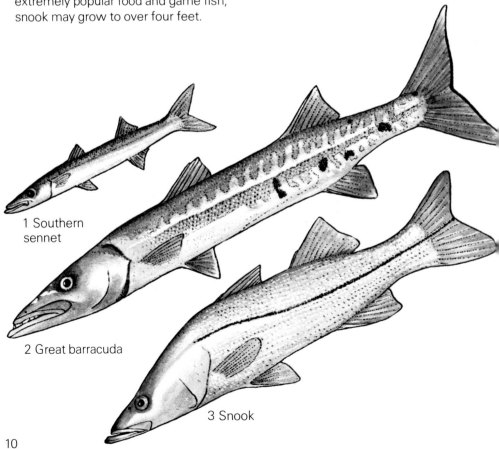

1 Southern sennet

2 Great barracuda

3 Snook

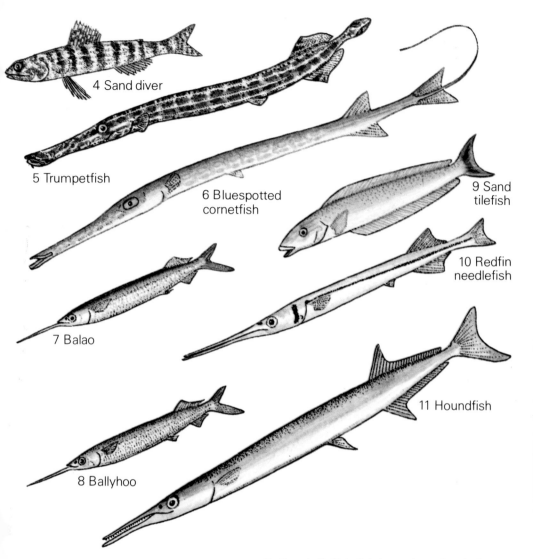

4 Sand diver

5 Trumpetfish

6 Bluespotted cornetfish

9 Sand tilefish

7 Balao

10 Redfin needlefish

8 Ballyhoo

11 Houndfish

9 **Sand tilefish** *(Malacanthus plumieri)* Hovering a few inches above its burrow, this tilefish dives in headfirst if disturbed. Length is two feet.

6 **Bluespotted cornetfish** *(Fistularia tabacaria)* Excluding the caudal whip length, this fish may grow to six feet.

7 **Balao** *(Hemiramphus balao)* The balao has a red-tipped lower jaw that is longer than the upper. This swift schooling fish grows to 15 inches.

8 **Ballyhoo** *(Hemiramphus brasiliensis)* Another halfbeak similar to the balao, ballyhoo differ in having orange at the tip of the beak and upper tail lobe.

10 **Redfin needlefish** *(Strongylura notata)* This fish has a long beak studded with many sharp teeth. It skims about the surface inshore, occasionally leaping into the air. Length is three feet.

11 **Houndfish** *(Tylosurus crocodilus)* Close to the redfin in appearance and habits, the houndfish grows to five feet. It is edible and has green teeth and bones.

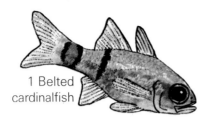

1 Belted cardinalfish

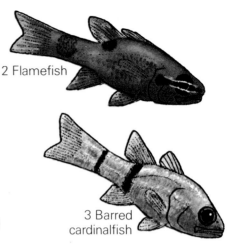

2 Flamefish

Cardinalfishes

3 Barred cardinalfish

1 **Belted cardinalfish** *(Apogon townsendi)* This tiny iridescent fish grows to almost three inches. Males incubate eggs orally.

2 **Flamefish** *(Apogon maculatus)* Large black eyes striped with white and black interrupt the vivid red on the five-inch flamefish.

3 **Barred cardinalfish** *(Apogon binotatus)* Ranging from red to pallid in hue, two narrow black bars remain constant to distinguish this fish, which reaches five inches.

Squirrelfishes*

4 **Longspine squirrelfish** *(Holocentrus rufus)* Marked with white spots near the margin of its spiny dorsal fin, this fish grows to over one foot.

5 **Squirrelfish** *(Holocentrus ascensionis)* The golden orange dorsal fin separates this 15-inch fish from its look-alike, the longspine squirrelfish.

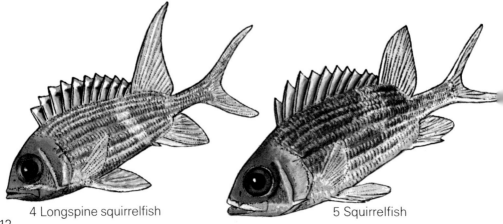

4 Longspine squirrelfish

5 Squirrelfish

6 **Dusky squirrelfish** *(Holocentrus vexillarius)* A broad black stripe between the first and third dorsal fin spines mark this six-inch squirrelfish. The dark red and white stripes on the upper half of the body are separated by fine black lines.

7 **Reef squirrelfish** *(Holocentrus coruscus)* The first three or four dorsal fin spines are marked by a black spot with whitish borders above and below. These black spots continue as a red stripe farther back on this small (5.5 inches) squirrelfish.

8 **Longjaw squirrelfish** *(Holocentrus marianus)* A projecting lower jaw and long anal fin spine that can reach to the tail base characterizes this eight-inch fish.

9 **Cardinal soldierfish** *(Plectrypops retrospinis)* This fish is all red. It grows to five inches.

10 **Blackbar soldierfish** *(Myripristis jacobus)* Named for the dark bar behind its head, the blackbar soldierfish can grow to eight inches.

*Squirrelfishes are generally considered edible, but their small size and spiny, prickly bodies discourage most people from eating them.

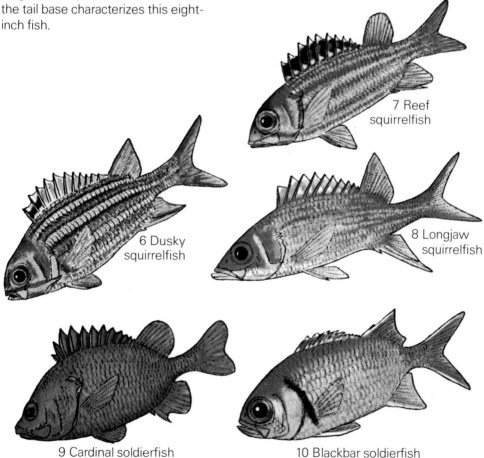

7 Reef squirrelfish

6 Dusky squirrelfish

8 Longjaw squirrelfish

9 Cardinal soldierfish

10 Blackbar soldierfish

Hamlets

Shy and retiring, these flamboyant-hued seabasses dart quickly away if startled. Ranging from five to six inches, they are functional hermaphrodites, with both eggs and sperm produced by each fish.

1 **Shy hamlet** *(Hypoplectrus guttavarius)*
2 **Indigo hamlet** *(Hypoplectrus indigo)*
3 **Barred hamlet** *(Hypoplectrus puella)*
4 **Blue hamlet** *(Hypoplectrus gemma)*
5 **Butter hamlet** *(Hypoplectrus unicolor)*

Basslets and seabasses

6 **Creole-fish** *(Paranthias furcifer)* Color varies from red-brown to salmon pink, but three white spots along the dorsal area remain constant. This fish may grow to over ten inches.

7 **Tobaccofish** *(Serranus tabacarius)* may reach about five inches.

8 **Fairy basslet** *(Gramma loreto)* Ready to dive into the nearest hole for safety, this three-inch fish often swims upside down under ledges and caves.

9 **Blackcap basslet** *(Gramma melacara)* A deep-water cousin of the fairy basslet, the blackcap grows to four inches.

10 **Peppermint bass** *(Liopropoma rubre)* Hiding in caves by day, the peppermint bass reaches to about three inches.

11 **Candy bass** *(Liopropoma carmabi)* A look-alike of the peppermint bass, the candy bass grows to about two inches.

12 **Harlequin bass** *(Serranus tigrinus)* Distinctive markings make this four-inch fish unmistakable.

Bigeyes

13 **Glasseye snapper** *(Priacanthus cruentatus)* Capable of rapid changes from deep or pale red to a striped silvery pattern, this foot-long fish is nocturnal.

14 **Bigeye** *(Priacanthus arenatus)* More constant in its red color and attaining a greater length of 15 inches, the bigeye is further distinguished from the glasseye by the dusky to black margins of the lower and tail fins.

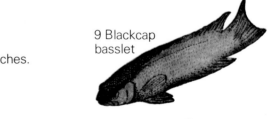
9 Blackcap basslet

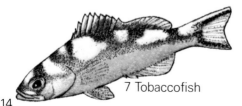
7 Tobaccofish

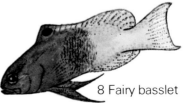
8 Fairy basslet

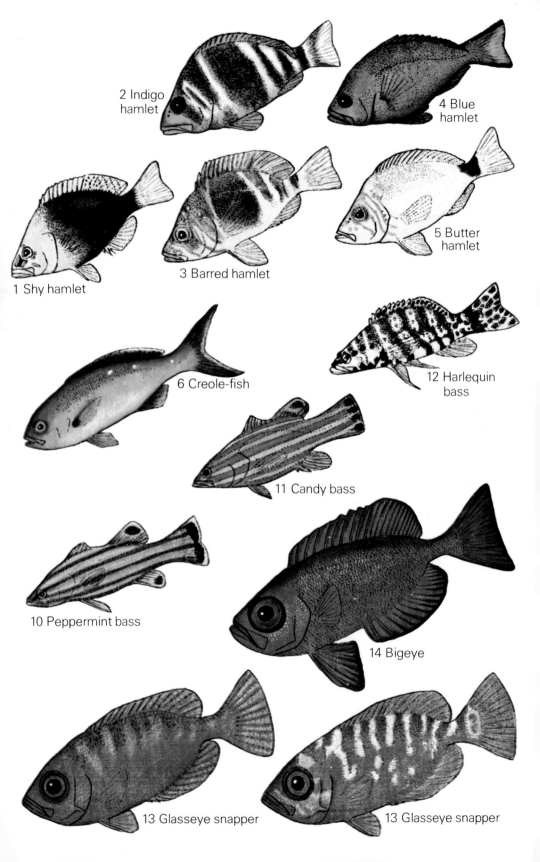

2 Indigo hamlet

4 Blue hamlet

1 Shy hamlet

3 Barred hamlet

5 Butter hamlet

6 Creole-fish

12 Harlequin bass

11 Candy bass

10 Peppermint bass

14 Bigeye

13 Glasseye snapper

13 Glasseye snapper

Jewfish and groupers

Highly variable, groupers may flash new colors and patterns during the transition from juvenile to adult, while moving from one site to another, or when startled. They also undergo great changes in their sexual development. All groupers mature first as females and produce eggs. They change sex later in life to become functional males. Groupers are bottom dwellers, hiding in caves and holes or swimming about close to the bottom.

1 **Jewfish** *(Epinephelus itajara)* Capable of providing enough food for a large banquet, this giant sea bass can be recognized by size alone. Jewfish can grow to eight feet and weigh 700 pounds.*

2 **Marbled grouper** *(Epinephelus inermis)* This steep-profiled grouper has been recorded at over two feet.*

3 **Black grouper** *(Mycteroperca bonaci)* This large food fish may attain four feet and weigh 150 pounds.*

4 **Tiger grouper** *(Mycteroperca tigris)* Well named for its markings, the tiger grouper reaches about three feet.*

5 **Yellowfin grouper** *(Mycteroperca venenosa)* Large individuals of this fish have caused fish poisoning (ciguatera). Yellowfin grouper can reach three feet.*

6 **Yellowmouth grouper** *(Mycteroperca interstitialis)* Named for the interior color of its mouth, this fish grows to less than three feet.*

7 **Red grouper** *(Epinephelus morio)* A look alike of the Nassau grouper, this fish lacks the black saddle on the tail base. This highly variable grouper is known to reach to three feet and over 50 pounds.*

8 **Nassau grouper** *(Epinephelus striatus)* In addition to the black saddle on the tail base, the Nassau is distinguished from the red grouper by the dark band running through the eye, five dark bars banding the body, and black dots that ring the eye. Larger than the red grouper it attains a length of four feet.*

*These fish are edible. Some large specimens can cause fish poisoning.

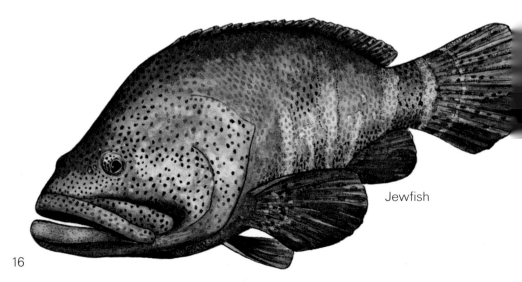

Jewfish

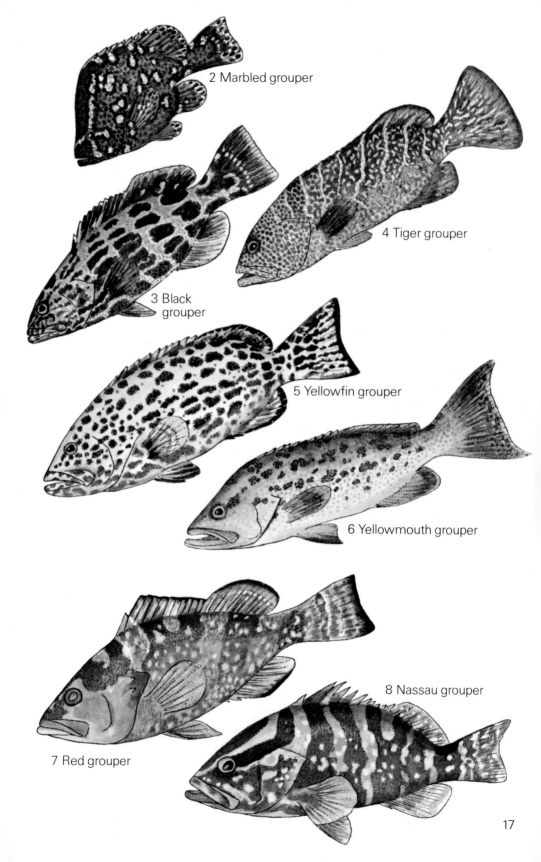

2 Marbled grouper

4 Tiger grouper

3 Black grouper

5 Yellowfin grouper

6 Yellowmouth grouper

8 Nassau grouper

7 Red grouper

17

Groupers continued

1 **Rock hind** *(Epinephelus adscensionis)*
Dark blotches on its back and a dark
saddle marking on the tail base help to
distinguish the rock hind from its close
relative, the red hind. These blotches
are composed of groups of heavily
pigmented spots. The rock hind may
exceed 18 inches.*

2 **Red hind** *(Epinephelus guttatus)*
Dusky margins on fins as indicated
and the discontinuance of the spotted
pattern on the tail further separate
the red hind from the rock hind. Size
is about the same, 18 inches.*

3 **Spotted soapfish** *(Rypticus
subbifrenatus)* Soapfishes are named
for the mucus coating on their bodies
that can cause a "sudsy" effect in the
water when these fish are handled.
The spotted soapfish grows to
about six inches.

4 **Greater soapfish** *(Rypticus saponaceus)*
The mucus on this species may be toxic,
perhaps affording some protection from
predation. This is the largest of the
soapfishes, reaching 13 inches.

5 **Graysby** *(Epinephelus cruentatus)*
One of the most variable seabasses,
the graysby may exhibit its
characteristic three (or four) back
spots as either black or white, with the
ground color going from almost white
to dark brown. Shown are two of the
more commonly seen patterns, but
the foot-long graysby can produce
many other color phases.*

6 **Coney** *(Epinephelus fulvus)* Two black
spots at the tip of the lower jaw and
two more at the tail base mark this fish.
Small body spots are usually blue, but
background coloring ranges from the red
and brown pictured to golden yellow or
olive. When excited, the coney may show
a bicolor effect, with the lower body
almost white and the upper quite dark.
Coneys grow to just over one foot.*

*These fish are edible. Some large
specimens can cause fish poisoning.

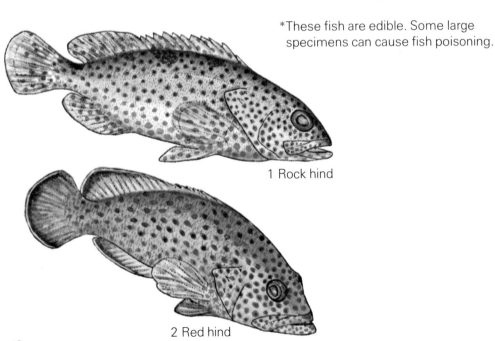

1 Rock hind

2 Red hind

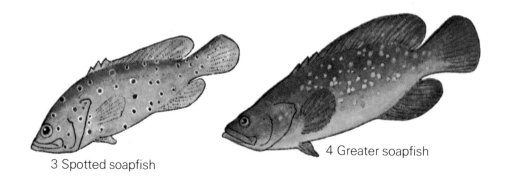

3 Spotted soapfish

4 Greater soapfish

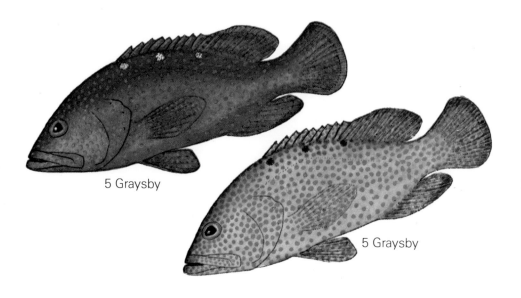

5 Graysby

5 Graysby

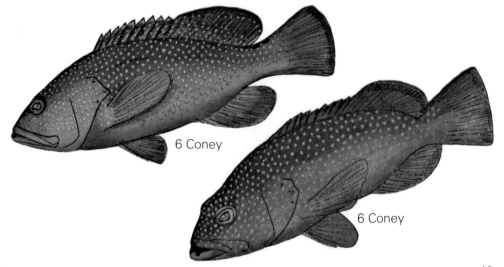

6 Coney

6 Coney

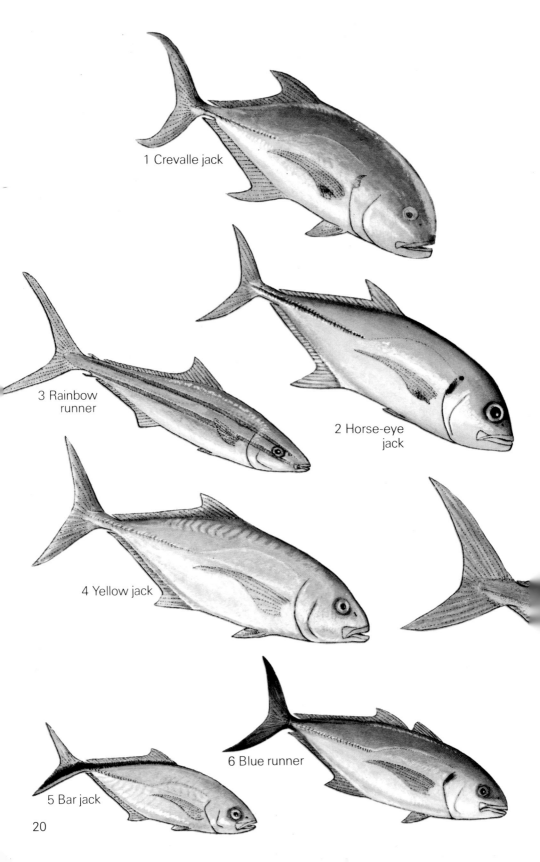

1 Crevalle jack

2 Horse-eye jack

3 Rainbow runner

4 Yellow jack

5 Bar jack

6 Blue runner

20

Jacks

1 **Crevalle jack** *(Caranx hippos)* A great game fish, as are most of the swift-swimming jacks, the crevalle grows to over three feet.*

2 **Horse-eye jack** *(Caranx latus)* Similar to the crevalle, this jack has a less steep profile, larger eye and probably does not exceed three feet.*

3 **Rainbow runner** *(Elagatis bipinnulata)* This slim, elongated jack of up to four feet long is a good food fish.

4 **Yellow jack** *(Caranx bartholomaei)* Another edible game fish, the yellow jack grows to about three feet.

5 **Bar jack** *(Caranx ruber)* Note the dark bar running from the dorsal area to the lower tail on this two-foot fish.*

6 **Blue runner** *(Caranx crysos)* Growing to over two feet, this is one of the best tasting jacks.

7 **Greater amberjack** *(Seriola dumerili)* Prized by sport fishermen, some members of this species may reach six feet and weigh 150 pounds.*

8 **African pompano** *(Alectis crinitus)* Trailing graceful fin rays that seem to mimic jellyfish, the African pompano attains about three feet.

*Large specimens of jacks may be poisonous to eat.

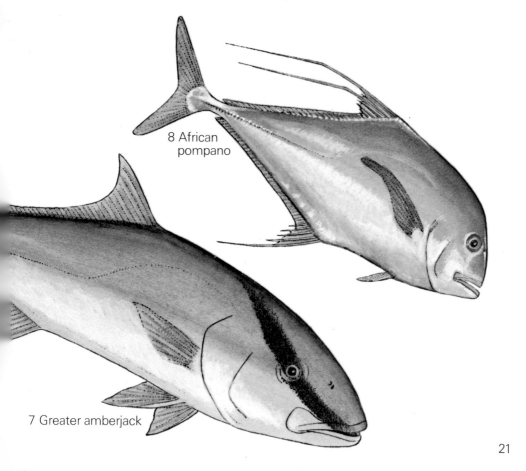

8 African pompano

7 Greater amberjack

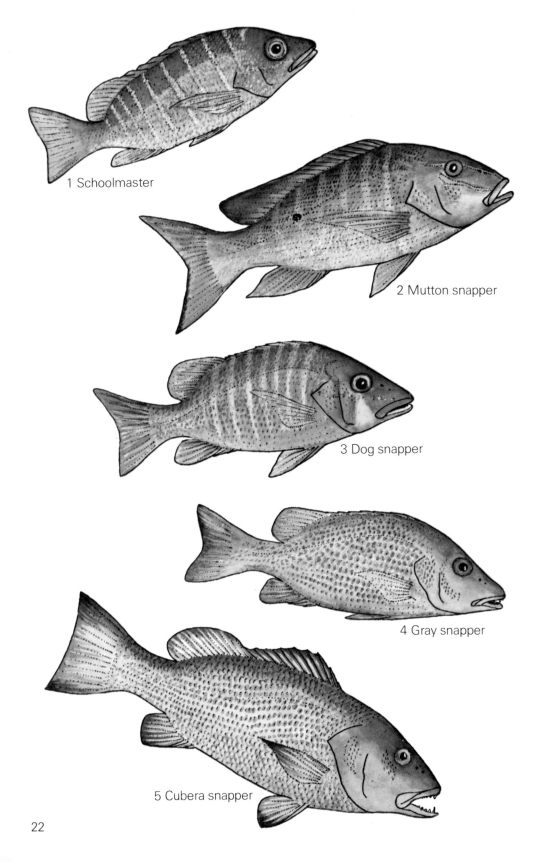

1 Schoolmaster

2 Mutton snapper

3 Dog snapper

4 Gray snapper

5 Cubera snapper

22

Snappers

1 Schoolmaster *(Lutjanus apodus)*
Looking most like the dog snapper (below), this fish lacks the triangular pale marking under the eye. An edible fish, the schoolmaster can grow to about two feet.

2 Mutton snapper *(Lutjanus analis)*
With vivid blue spots and lines around the eye, a dark spot on the back and a black-edged tail, the mutton snapper is further distinguished by having a pointed anal fin. A good food fish, it grows to 30 inches.

3 Dog snapper *(Lutjanus jocu)* Though not always present, the pale triangular area below the eye most readily identifies the 30-inch-long dog snapper. Opinion on its edibility is divided, and in some areas the flesh may be poisonous.

4 Gray snapper *(Lutjanus griseus)*
Found on the open reef or inshore near mangrove-ringed creeks, the gray snapper may be reddish as shown, or gray-to-brown. This two-foot fish is very good eating.

5 Cubera snapper *(Lutjanus cyanopterus)*
Though nearly all snappers have enlarged canine teeth, the cubera, at a length of up to four feet and a weight of 100 pounds, seems to be all teeth. Danger lies more in the teeth of one who eats this fish, as it may sometimes be poisonous.

6 Lane snapper *(Lutjanus synagris)*
Sometimes seen in schools, this 15-inch fish is delicious to eat.

7 Mahogany snapper *(Lutjanus mahogoni)*
Commonly seen as a pale silvery fish over the reef, mahogany snappers may sometimes have an overall reddish tinge. Fins on this 15-inch fish are almost always edged with dark red.

8 Yellowtail snapper *(Ocyurus chrysurus)*
This highly esteemed food fish reaches a length of 30 inches.

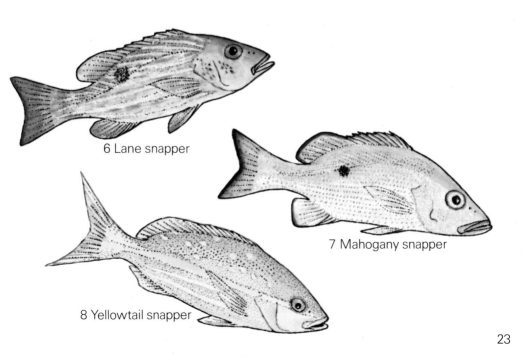

6 Lane snapper

7 Mahogany snapper

8 Yellowtail snapper

Grunts

Named for the sounds they are able to produce, grunts are an important food fish family.

1 **Smallmouth grunt**
Haemulon chrysargyreum
Grows to nine inches.

2 **Tomtate**
Haemulon aurolineatum
Up to nine inches. Note dark mark at tail base.

3 **French grunt**
Haemulon flavolineatum
To about one foot.

4 **Black grunt**
Haemulon bonariense
Less than one foot.

5 **Sailors choice**
Haemulon parrai
To about 15 inches.

6 **Caesar grunt**
Haemulon carbonarium
Over one foot.

7 **Cottonwick**
Haemulon melanurum
Grows to 12 inches. Note diagonal stripe from back to tail.

8 **Spanish grunt**
Haemulon macrostomum
May reach 18 inches.

9 **Bluestriped grunt**
Haemulon sciurus
Up to 18 inches.

10 **White grunt**
Haemulon plumieri
Length is about 16 inches.

11 **Porkfish**
Anisotremus virginicus
Over one foot.

12 **Black margate**
Anisotremus surinamensis
Over two feet.

13 **Margate**
Haemulon album
Over two feet.

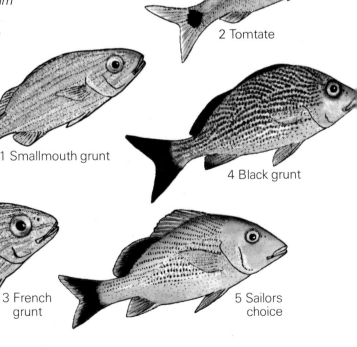

2 Tomtate

1 Smallmouth grunt

4 Black grunt

3 French grunt

5 Sailors choice

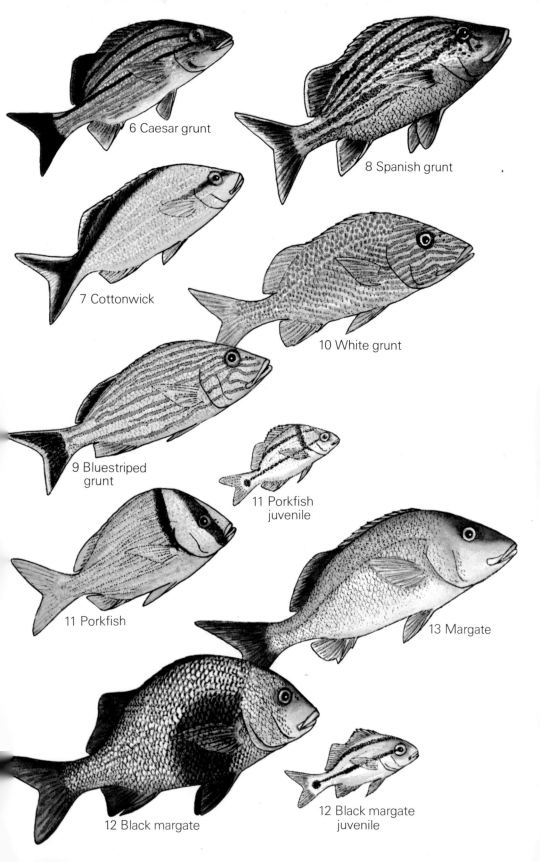

6 Caesar grunt

8 Spanish grunt

7 Cottonwick

10 White grunt

9 Bluestriped grunt

11 Porkfish juvenile

11 Porkfish

13 Margate

12 Black margate

12 Black margate juvenile

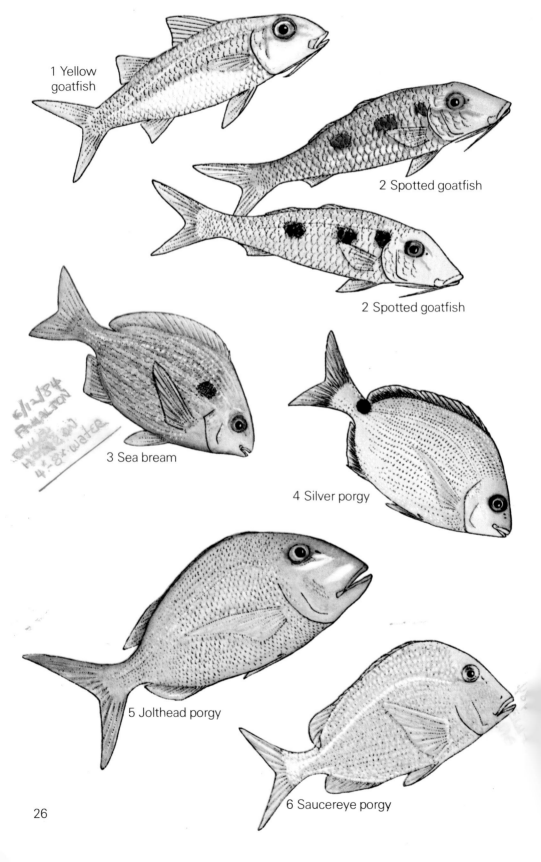

1 Yellow goatfish

2 Spotted goatfish

2 Spotted goatfish

3 Sea bream

4 Silver porgy

5 Jolthead porgy

6 Saucereye porgy

6/12/84
FINALSON
BLUFF
HORIZON
4'-8' water

26

Goatfishes

1 **Yellow goatfish** *(Mulloidichthys mart-inicus)* probes the sand or mud bottom at night with its sensitive chin barbels in search of food. This fish assumes many color changes. When on seagrass beds it may be greenish, on sandy bottom, pale. The most constant feature is a yellow body stripe that widens to cover the tail fin. Reaching to about one foot, this is a highly esteemed food fish.*

2 **Spotted goatfish** *(Pseudupeneus maculatus)* Another chameleon of the ocean, this fish has three dark blotches instead of the stripe, and a longer snout than the yellow goatfish. Similar in its use of barbels to root out food, the spotted goatfish feeds by day. Length is up to ten inches.*

Porgies

3 **Sea bream** *(Archosargus rhomboidalis)* A shallow-water fish, the sea bream may grow to one foot.*

4 **Silver porgy** *(Diplodus argenteus)* With the typical flattened porgy body and small mouth, the silver porgy is set apart by a black saddle on its tail fin. Length is about one foot.*

5 **Jolthead porgy** *(Calamus bajonado)* This silvery, iridescent fish is the largest of the inshore porgies, attaining over two feet. Two dominant white bands mark the cheek area.*

6 **Saucereye porgy** *(Calamus calamus)* Most often seen as a silvery iridescent fish, the saucereye may also show a blotched pattern. Yellow spots mark the blue cheek on this 15-inch porgy.*

Drums

7 **Sand drum** *(Umbrina coroides)* Called "croakers" or "drums" because of the sounds they are able to produce, this family inhabits shallow water. The sand drum features a single barbel on its chin. Length is up to one foot.*

8 **Reef croaker** *(Odontoscion dentex)* Hiding by day and feeding by night, this fish grows to less than one foot.*

*These fish are edible.

7 Sand drum

8 Reef croaker

Drums continued

1 **Jackknife fish** *(Equetus lanceolatus)*
Cutting a swath with its elongated front dorsal fin as it swims, the jackknife fish inhabits deeper waters than others of its genus. While the nine-inch adults are distinctive, young of this species are often mistaken for the juvenile spotted drum.

2 **Spotted drum** *(Equetus punctatus)*
A secretive reef fish, the spotted drum is much sought by aquarists. Sporting pale spots and more than one body stripe, adults are unmistakable. Young are set apart from the look-alike juvenile jackknife fish by the black spot that marks the snout. Spotted drums are said to reach one foot.

3 **Highhat** *(Equetus acuminatus)*
Confusion reigns over the common and scientific names of this fish. Variously known as the striped drum and *Equetus pulcher,* it is related to the cubbyu, *Equetus umbrosus.* The highhat may grow to nine inches.

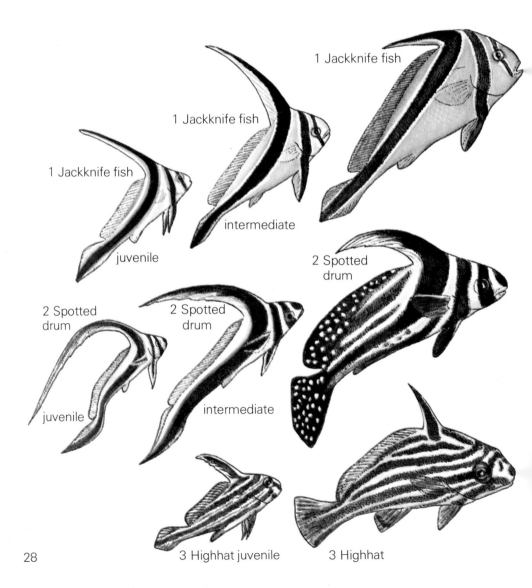

1 Jackknife fish

1 Jackknife fish

1 Jackknife fish

intermediate

juvenile

2 Spotted drum

2 Spotted drum

2 Spotted drum

juvenile

intermediate

3 Highhat juvenile

3 Highhat

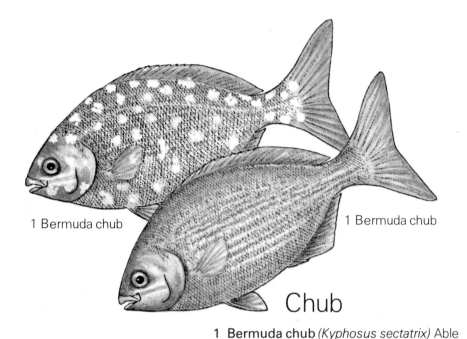

1 Bermuda chub

1 Bermuda chub

Chub

1 **Bermuda chub** *(Kyphosus sectatrix)* Able to adjust to a variety of backgrounds by changing from light to dark or assuming an overall spotted pattern, the Bermuda chub is chiefly herbivorous. Once a leading food fish, the flesh is highly variable in taste, and is no longer sought after for the table. Length is up to 18 inches.

Flounder

2 **Peacock flounder** *(Bothus lunatus)* All flatfishes start life symmetrically. Within days after hatching, one eye migrates to the other on the upper side of the body. At that time, the fish settles down to its bottom-dwelling existence. This fish is extremely well camouflaged and highly edible.

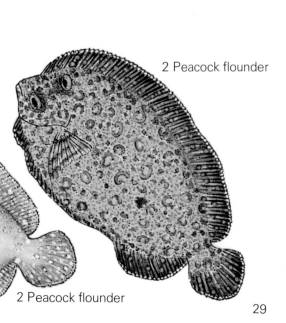

2 Peacock flounder

2 Peacock flounder

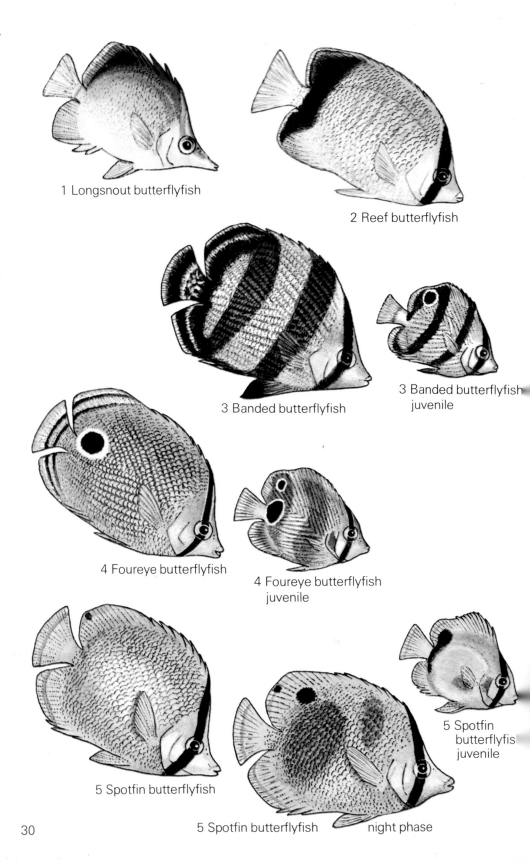

1 Longsnout butterflyfish

2 Reef butterflyfish

3 Banded butterflyfish

3 Banded butterflyfish juvenile

4 Foureye butterflyfish

4 Foureye butterflyfish juvenile

5 Spotfin butterflyfish juvenile

5 Spotfin butterflyfish

5 Spotfin butterflyfish night phase

Butterflyfishes

1 **Longsnout butterflyfish** (*Prognathodes aculeatus*) Poking its elongated snout into crevices and among sea urchin spines, the longsnout butterflyfish searches out the small invertebrates that make up its diet. This tiny (just over three inches long) species inhabits deep water, but is sometimes seen in shallows.

2 **Reef butterflyfish** (*Chaetodon sedentarius*) An eye-concealing stripe running down the face of most butterflyfish makes it difficult to guess which way they are headed. The reef butterflyfish sports another dark band at the rear of its squarish body. Length is six inches.

3 **Banded butterflyfish** (*Chaetodon striatus*) The six-inch banded butterflyfish furthers the directional confusion of its eye stripe by adding four more bold dark bands. Like most butterflyfish, adults usually travel in pairs.

4 **Foureye butterflyfish** (*Chaetodon capistratus*) A set of false "eyes" ringed with white, and dark lines marking the scale rows distinguish the foureye butterflyfish. Maximum size is six inches.

5 **Spotfin butterflyfish** (*Chaetodon ocellatus*) The most distinctive feature of this fish is the small black mark on the edge of the soft dorsal fin. A larger black spot appears in its night phase, in addition to diffuse dusky bars. Size ranges up to seven or eight inches.

Spadefish

6 **Atlantic spadefish** (*Chaetodipterus faber*) When tiny and almost entirely black, spadefish mimic drifting plant debris by floating on one side near shore. Upon assuming the barred-silver adult phase, they swim upright and often form large schools. Any spadefish over 18 inches long is exceptional, but they may reach up to three feet and weigh 20 pounds. The flesh is tasty.

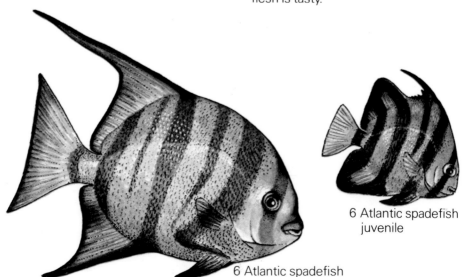

6 Atlantic spadefish juvenile

6 Atlantic spadefish

Angelfishes

Angelfishes are the most curious fish on the reef. Their often gaudy colors blend in surprisingly well as they flutter among sea fans or nibble on bright-hued sponges. Immature angels, marked with color patterns different from adults, sometimes augment their diet with parasites they remove from other fish.

1 **Blue angelfish** *(Holacanthus bermudensis)* Similar to the queen angelfish (below), the blue lacks its crown and all yellow tail. Both these angelfishes grow to 18 inches. Juveniles of these two species are even more alike, and are set apart by the degree of curvature on the stripes of the juvenile queen angelfish.

2 **Queen angelfish** *(Holacanthus ciliaris)* Garbed in a galaxy of colors, the queen angelfish derives its imperial status from the crown on its nape.

3 **Cherubfish** *(Centropyge argi)*
4 **Flameback cherubfish** *(Centropyge aurantonotus)* These pygmy angelfishes grow to less than three inches.

5 **Rock beauty** *(Holacanthus tricolor)* The discus-shaped body features a dark spot that increases in size as the fish grows to its ultimate length of one foot.

6 **French angelfish** *(Pomacanthus paru)* In basic black with a yellow scallop on each scale, the French angelfish has a rounded tail fin in all stages of growth. It reaches one foot.

7 **Gray angelfish** *(Pomacanthus arcuatus)* Velvety shades of gray and a straight-edged tail distinguish this fish from the French angelfish. Length is two feet.

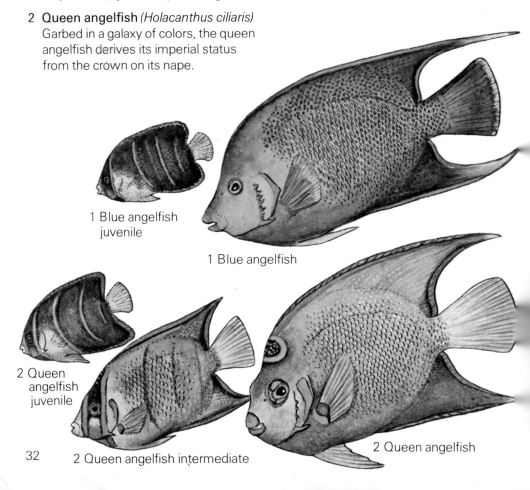

1 Blue angelfish juvenile

1 Blue angelfish

2 Queen angelfish juvenile

2 Queen angelfish

2 Queen angelfish intermediate

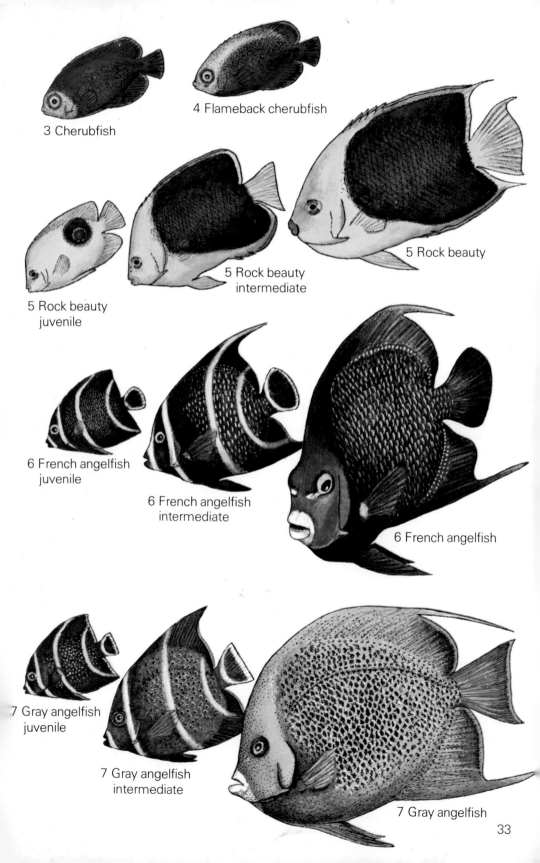

3 Cherubfish

4 Flameback cherubfish

5 Rock beauty juvenile

5 Rock beauty intermediate

5 Rock beauty

6 French angelfish juvenile

6 French angelfish intermediate

6 French angelfish

7 Gray angelfish juvenile

7 Gray angelfish intermediate

7 Gray angelfish

Damselfishes

Small but pugnacious damselfishes will nip at large fish or even divers when their territory is threatened. The male usually stands guard over the dark red to purple egg clusters lest they be eaten by other fish. Damselfishes are rarely used as food fish.

1 **Night sergeant** *(Abudefduf taurus)* Wary of intruders, the night sergeant stays close to the bottom of the turbulent shallow water it inhabits. This largest of all damselfishes grows to ten inches.

2 **Sergeant major** *(Abudefduf saxatilis)* This fish may show a pale phase when swimming freely or over a sandy bottom, or a dark phase when seeking shelter among coral crevices. It is seen everywhere on the reef and grows to about five inches. Similar in appearance to the night sergeant, the sergeant major has more sharply defined bars.

3 **Beaugregory** *(Pomacentrus leucostictus)* One of several species with electric blue spots and lines on its head and back, the beaugregory becomes dusky in hue as it reaches to slightly over four inches.

4 **Cocoa damselfish** *(Pomacentrus variabilis)* Easily mistaken for the beaugregory, the cocoa damselfish differs in usually having a dark spot at the tail base. This fish also turns dusky when it reaches about four inches.

5 **Threespot damselfish** *(Pomacentrus planifrons)* Deeper bodied than other damselfish, the threespot lacks the blue markings of the beaugregory and cocoa damselfish. While juveniles show three dark spots, the dorsal spot is lost in adults. Size is just over four inches.

6 **Bicolor damselfish** *(Pomacentrus partitus)* Distinguished from all other damselfishes by its darkened front and pale rear, the bicolor differs as well in lacking spots or lines anywhere except for the dark mark on its pectoral fin base. There is much variation in the boundary between dark and light on this three-inch fish.

7 **Yellowtail damselfish** *(Microspathodon chrysurus)* Body color may vary, but metallic blue spots mark this fish. Adults (growing to about seven inches long) may show relatively smaller and fewer dots than juveniles. Tail color is yellow on all but the smallest size yellowtail damselfish.

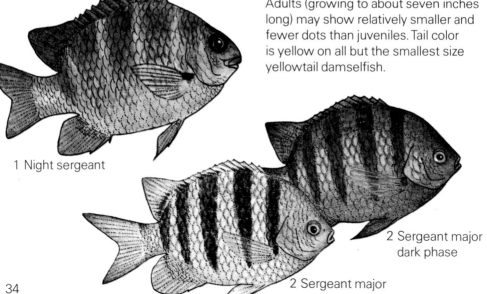

1 Night sergeant

2 Sergeant major
dark phase

2 Sergeant major

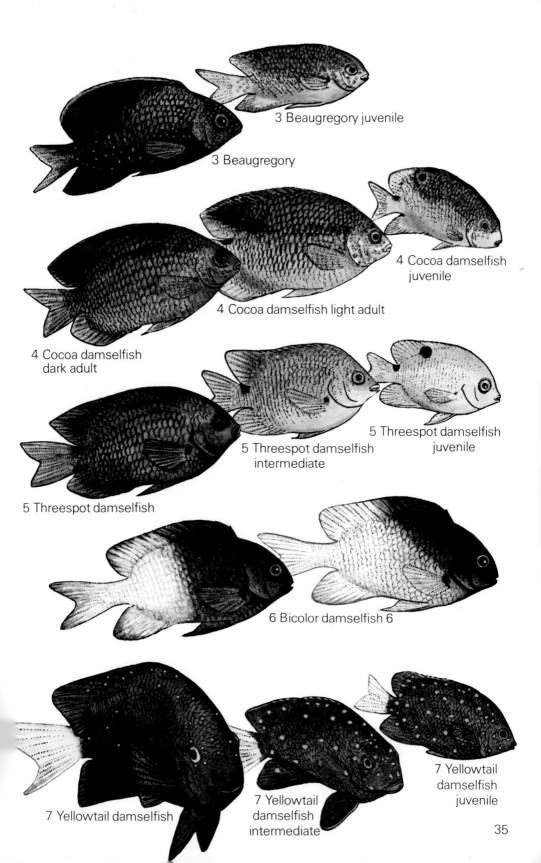

3 Beaugregory juvenile

3 Beaugregory

4 Cocoa damselfish juvenile

4 Cocoa damselfish light adult

4 Cocoa damselfish dark adult

5 Threespot damselfish juvenile

5 Threespot damselfish intermediate

5 Threespot damselfish

6 Bicolor damselfish 6

7 Yellowtail damselfish juvenile

7 Yellowtail damselfish

7 Yellowtail damselfish intermediate

35

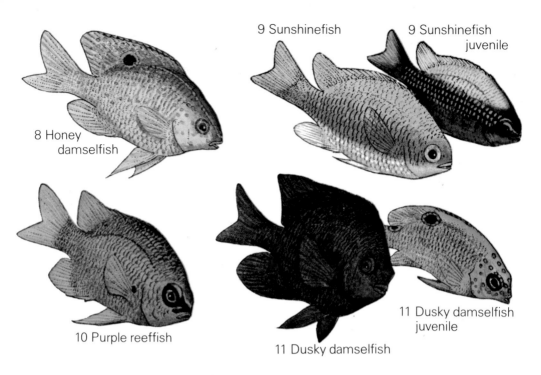

9 Sunshinefish

9 Sunshinefish juvenile

8 Honey damselfish

10 Purple reeffish

11 Dusky damselfish

11 Dusky damselfish juvenile

Damselfishes continued

8 **Honey damselfish** *(Pomacentrus mellis)* have a large dark spot on the base of the dorsal fin, which makes them unmistakable. Length is to three inches.

9 **Sunshinefish** *(Chromis insolatus)* grow to about four inches long and inhabit deeper water than most damselfishes.

10 **Purple reeffish** *(Chromis scotti)* are closely related to sunshinefish and also grow to about four inches.

11 **Dusky damselfish** *(Pomacentrus fuscus)* are brilliantly colored as juveniles. Adult color may be grayish-brown to black. Length is about four inches.

12 **Blue chromis** *(Chromis cyaneus)* swim in large numbers, often accompanied by brown chromis. Note dark margins on the tail and dorsal fin of this five-inch fish.

13 **Brown chromis** *(Chromis multilineatus)* has pale tips on the dorsal and tail fins, and also features a dark blotch at the pectoral-fin base. This six-inch fish feeds on plankton.

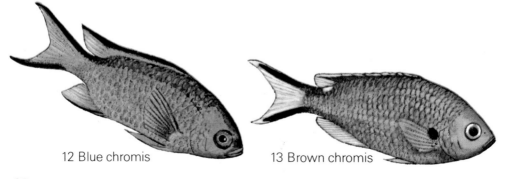

12 Blue chromis

13 Brown chromis

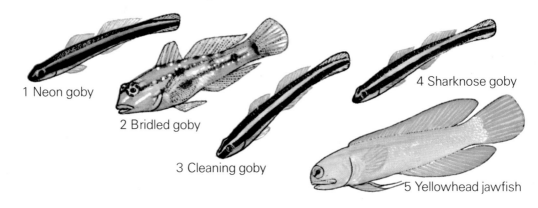

1 Neon goby

2 Bridled goby

3 Cleaning goby

4 Sharknose goby

5 Yellowhead jawfish

Gobies

Bright markings on these two-inch gobies attract other fish to the cleaning stations set up by them. Gobies gain a free meal of parasites for the service.

1 **Neon goby** (*Gobiosoma oceanops*)
3 **Cleaning goby** (*Gobiosoma genie*)
4 **Sharknose goby** (*Gobiosoma evelynae*)

2 **Bridled goby** (*Coryphopterus glauco-fraenum*) burrows its translucent body in sandy bottom. Size is three inches.

Jawfish

5 **Yellowhead jawfish** (*Opistognathus aurifrons*) turns slowly above its burrow, feeding on small organisms passing by. Length is almost four inches.

Blenny

6 **Redlip blenny** (*Ophioblennius atlanticus*) may grow to almost five inches.

Sweeper

7 **Glassy sweeper** (*Pempheris schomburgki*) lends a coppery luster to the caves and hollows it inhabits. Size is six inches.

Hawkfish

8 **Redspotted hawkfish** (*Amblycirrhitus pinos*) often balances on its pectoral fins over coral. Size reached is less than four inches.

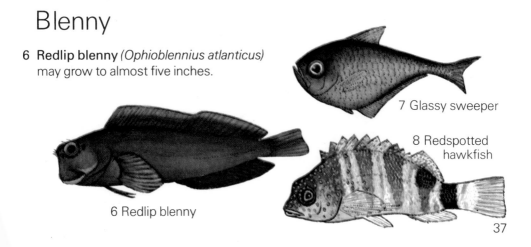

6 Redlip blenny

7 Glassy sweeper

8 Redspotted hawkfish

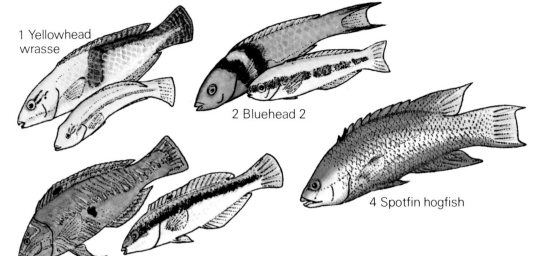

1 Yellowhead wrasse

2 Bluehead 2

4 Spotfin hogfish

3 Clown wrasse 3

Wrasses

Though this large family is extremely diverse, most wrasses are shaped like a flattened cigar and sport "buckteeth." They seem to be dragging their tails behind them as they cruise, propelled mainly by their pectoral fins. Wrasses undergo many changes in color and shape during the growth process. A small number of males of some species, possibly sex-reversed females, reach a phase known as supermales. They develop brighter colors and attain larger size. Wrasses are generally not good eating.

1 **Yellowhead wrasse** *(Halichoeres garnoti)* afford a splendid example of sex-linked changes in coloration. Adult males grow to about eight inches and are distinguished from females by the dark bar and stripe on their sides.

2 **Bluehead** *(Thalassoma bifasciatum)* have been observed in parasite-picking behavior when young. The supermale may grow to six inches. Immature males and females all show the yellow, striped color phase.

3 **Clown wrasse** *(Halichoeres maculipinna)* attains a length of about six inches.

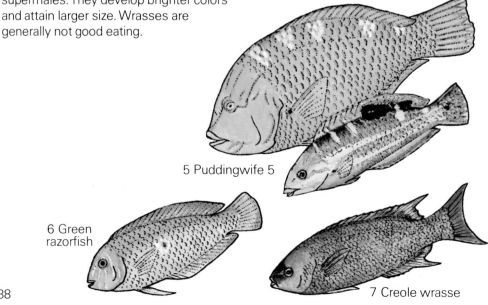

5 Puddingwife 5

6 Green razorfish

7 Creole wrasse

4 Spotfin hogfish *(Bodianus pulchellus)* can reach eight or nine inches.

5 Puddingwife *(Halichoeres radiatus)* adult males vary greatly from intermediate-size individuals. Reaching a length of 20 inches, this is the largest of its genus.

6 Green razorfish *(Hemipteronotus splendens)* attain a length of about five inches and are known to bite when handled. Note the steep forehead.

7 Creole wrasse *(Clepticus parrai)* have blue teeth and bones. This schooling fish can grow to one foot.

8 Spanish hogfish *(Bodianus rufus)* may reach two feet in length. Juveniles are parasite cleaners for other fish.

9 Hogfish *(Lachnolaimus maximus)* change color to suit background and activity, but three trailing dorsal fin spines identify them. Large adult males have a long, piglike snout. Alone among the wrasses, hogfish are much esteemed as food. Size is up to three feet.

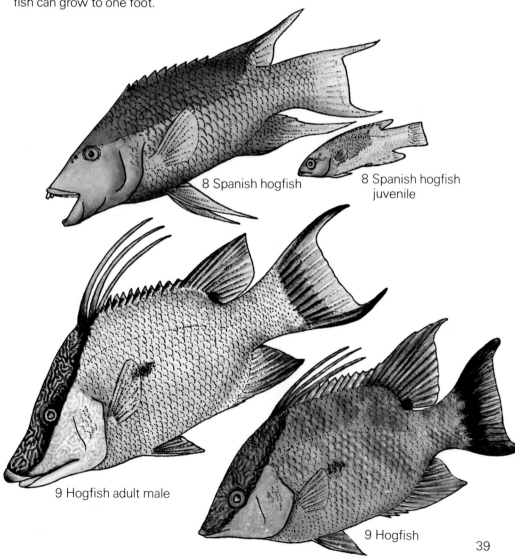

8 Spanish hogfish

8 Spanish hogfish juvenile

9 Hogfish adult male

9 Hogfish

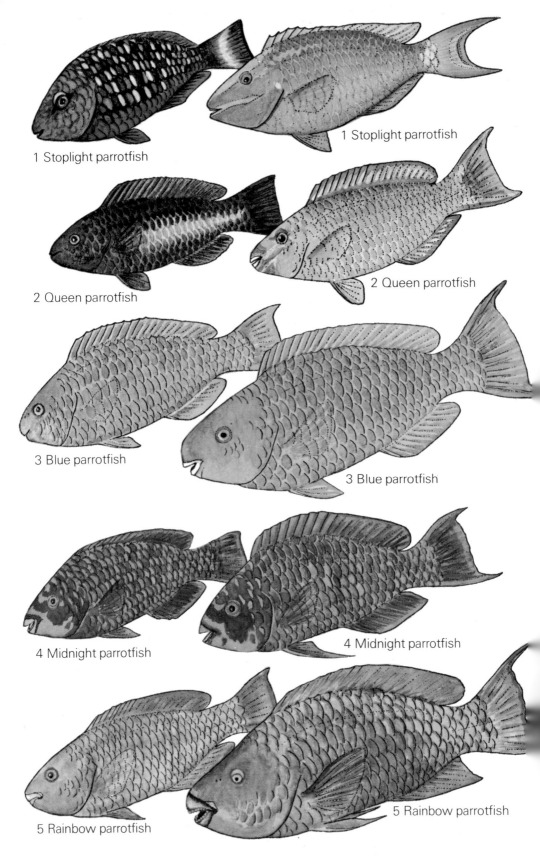

1 Stoplight parrotfish

1 Stoplight parrotfish

2 Queen parrotfish

2 Queen parrotfish

3 Blue parrotfish

3 Blue parrotfish

4 Midnight parrotfish

4 Midnight parrotfish

5 Rainbow parrotfish

5 Rainbow parrotfish

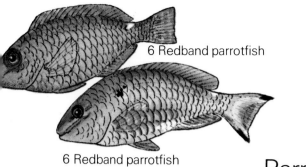

6 Redband parrotfish

6 Redband parrotfish

Parrotfishes

An efficient recycling machine, parrotfishes turn coral and rock into fine sand in the process of grazing algae from them. Females and males of most species are differently colored. In those with a shared color pattern, an occasional male attains larger size and more brilliant color and is called a terminal-phase male, or supermale. The flesh of parrotfishes spoils quickly and is not usually eaten. The blue parrotfish is sometimes poisonous.

Stoplight parrotfish *(Sparisoma viride)* Note the round yellow spot on the gill cover and the yellow tail base on the adult male. Red-phase individuals are unmistakable. Size reached is 20 inches.

Queen parrotfish *(Scarus vetula)* Drab-phase males and females differ from the adult male in both color and tail shape. Adult males grow to two feet.

Blue parrotfish *(Scarus coeruleus)* Large adults (perhaps only males) develop a hump on the forehead. They are said to reach a length of up to four feet.

4 **Midnight parrotfish** *(Scarus coelestinus)* feature green teeth, as do the rainbow parrotfish. Size reached is 30 inches.

5 **Rainbow parrotfish** *(Scarus guacamaia)* Adult males may grow to four feet and are extremely heavy-bodied.

6 **Redband parrotfish** *(Sparisoma aurofrenatum)* are small, reaching about 11 inches. The white tail saddle is distinctive, as are the dark markings on the adult male.

7 **Striped parrotfish** *(Scarus croicensis)* grows to less than one foot.

8 **Princess parrotfish** *(Scarus taeniopterus)* Note the yellow mid-body blotch on the adult male. Size is about 13 inches.

7 Striped parrotfish

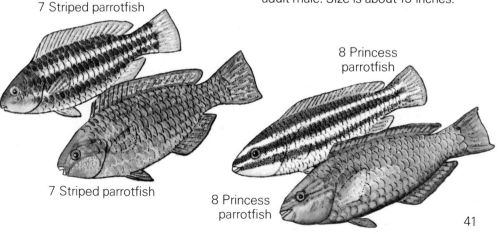

8 Princess parrotfish

7 Striped parrotfish

8 Princess parrotfish

Triggerfishes

Tough-skinned triggerfishes are able to view an intruder with one eye and, with the other, locate a convenient crevice to dive into. Once inside, they raise the first dorsal spine (locking it erect with a "trigger" device in the second spine), lower the pelvis and become firmly wedged in. Powerful jaws and sharp teeth enable them to eat invertebrates despite their small mouth. Triggerfishes can eat sea urchins with no damage to their eyes, which are set well back from the mouth. These fish are usually edible. The best tasting is the queen triggerfish which is sometimes, but rarely, poisonous.

1 **Queen triggerfish** *(Balistes vetula)* Electric blue "smile lines" and elongated fin rays mark this otherwise color-variable fish. Size is up to about two feet.

2 **Gray triggerfish** *(Balistes capriscus)* may reach about one foot.

3 **Ocean triggerfish** *(Canthidermis sufflamen)* can grow to two feet.

4 **Black durgon** *(Melichthys niger)* is basically black, outlined with pale streaks. Length is up to 20 inches.

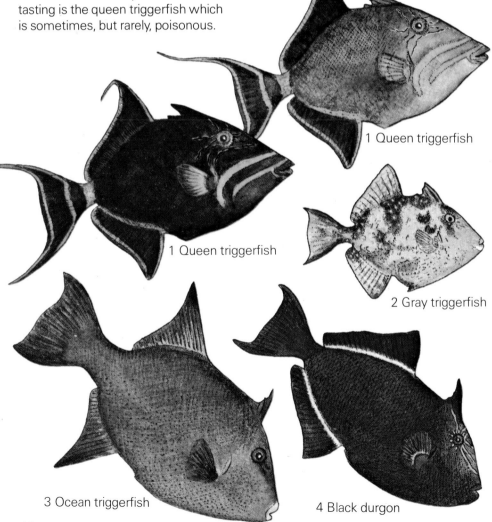

1 Queen triggerfish

1 Queen triggerfish

2 Gray triggerfish

3 Ocean triggerfish

4 Black durgon

Surgeonfishes carry a concealed weapon. Within the sheath at either side of the tail base is a hinged, lancetlike spine. Intruders may be threatened by a display of the sweeping tail, or actually slashed by the sharp spine. Surgeonfishes grow to just over one foot. They are poor eating and have been known to cause ciguatera (fish poisoning).

Blue tang (*Acanthurus coeruleus*) sports a light colored sheath for its spine. Dark wavy lines run lengthwise on the body and fins. Of the surgeonfishes shown, this species alone has young which differ greatly in color from the adults.

Surgeonfishes

2 Doctorfish (*Acanthurus chirurgus*) always show ten or more vertical brown bars on the side of the body. Doctorfish change from a light phase when over sandy bottom to a dark phase over the reef.

3 Ocean surgeon (*Acanthurus bahianus*) are changeable in color like the doctorfish, but the bright blue lines radiating from the eye remain constant. Note the crescent-shaped tail.

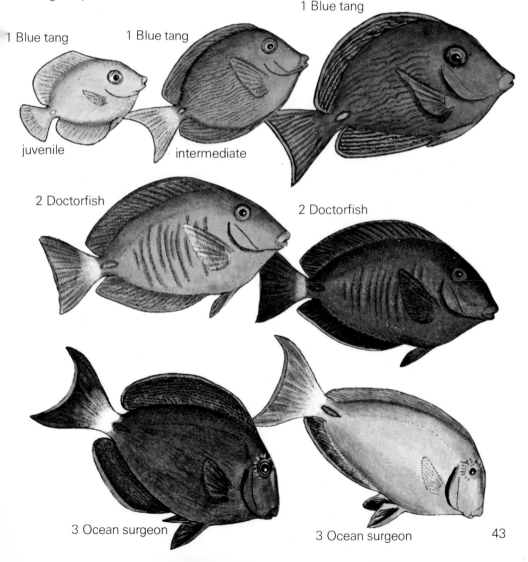

1 Blue tang

1 Blue tang

1 Blue tang

1 Blue tang

juvenile

intermediate

2 Doctorfish

2 Doctorfish

3 Ocean surgeon

3 Ocean surgeon

43

Filefishes

1 **Whitespotted filefish** *(Cantherhines macrocerus)* Capable of rapid changes from solid color to the white-spotted phase its name is derived from, this filefish features a black tail. Traveling in pairs (perhaps male and female), it feeds on sponges, stinging coral and other seemingly unwholesome fare. Length attained is about 17 inches.

2 **Orange filefish** *(Aluterus schoepfi)* Varying color to match the background, the orange filefish always retains its small orange spots. Size is two feet.

3 **Scrawled filefish** *(Aluterus scriptus)* Dots and dashes of bright blue punctuated by black spots call for attention, yet this fish blends into the seascape as it drifts in search of food. Size ranges to three feet.

4 **Orangespotted filefish** *(Cantherhines pullus)* Orange spots with brown centers mark this under-eight-inch filefish.

5 **Pygmy filefish** *(Monacanthus setifer)* usually show a mottled pattern, but can also assume an almost uniform shade of gray when over a sandy bottom. Maximum length is about seven inches.

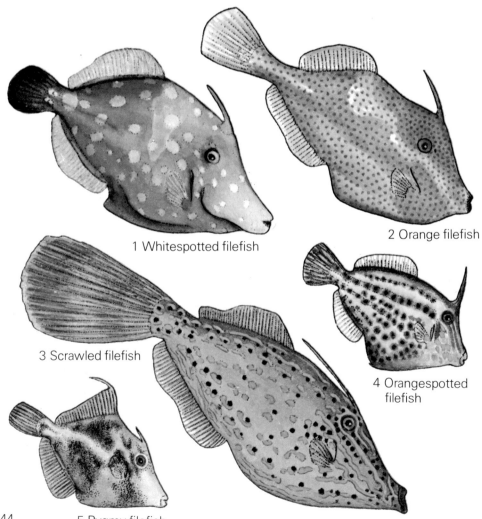

1 Whitespotted filefish

2 Orange filefish

3 Scrawled filefish

4 Orangespotted filefish

5 Pygmy filefish

Enclosed in an armor of bony plates with gaps for the mouth, eyes, nostrils, anus and fins, trunkfishes are unique. When under stress, they can secrete a substance toxic enough to kill other fish. Failure to clean the flesh properly before eating may cause illness from traces of this toxin.

1 **Honeycomb cowfish** (*Lactophrys polygonia*) Hornlike spines project from the eyes on this and the scrawled cowfish. Both grow to about 18 inches.

2 **Scrawled cowfish** (*Lactophrys quadricornis*) Note the parallel stripes on the cheek.

Trunkfishes

3 **Spotted trunkfish** (*Lactophrys bicaudalis*) Three white areas behind the eye interrupt the overall spots on the carapace. Length is about 18 inches.

4 **Smooth trunkfish** (*Lactophrys triqueter*) feed on burrowing organisms, sometimes "spitting" jets of water into the sand to uncover them. Length is under one foot.

5 **Trunkfish** (*Lactophrys trigonus*) usually show chainlike markings on the body, but some large individuals develop a dark, reticulate pattern. Length is 18 inches.

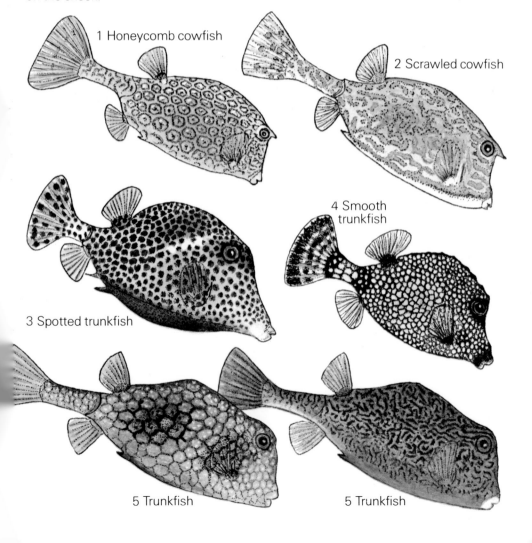

1 Honeycomb cowfish

2 Scrawled cowfish

4 Smooth trunkfish

3 Spotted trunkfish

5 Trunkfish

5 Trunkfish

When threatened, these scaleless fish balloon themselves up to three times normal size by drawing water into the abdomen. This ability, plus a tough spinous or prickly skin, may deter many predators from swallowing them. Strong, beaklike jaws enable puffers to crush and eat hard-shell invertebrates. Some puffers are considered a delicacy in Japan, though internal organs contain a powerful poison. When improperly cleaned, puffers are deadly to eat.

Burrfishes

1 Striped burrfish *(Chilomycterus schoepfi)* "Jet-propelled" by bursts of water forced through gill openings, the striped burrfish is further differentiated by meandering parallel lines on the body. Length is about ten inches.

2 Web burrfish *(Chilomycterus antillarum)* A webbed pattern marks this foot-long fish. Both the web and striped burrfish have short, permanently erect spines.

Porcupinefishes

3 Porcupinefish *(Diodon hystrix)* Largest of the spiny puffers at three feet, the porcupinefish also has the longest spines. These spines are erect only when the fish is inflated.

1 Striped burrfish

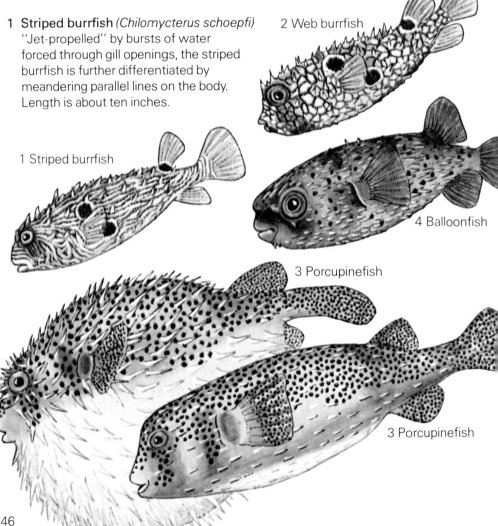

2 Web burrfish

4 Balloonfish

3 Porcupinefish

3 Porcupinefish

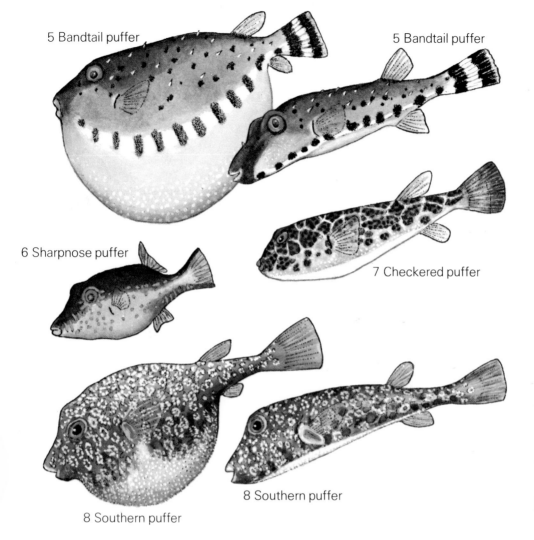

5 Bandtail puffer

5 Bandtail puffer

6 Sharpnose puffer

7 Checkered puffer

8 Southern puffer

8 Southern puffer

Balloonfish *(Diodon holocanthus),* like the porcupinefish, have spines that are movable. Color and size set them apart. Balloonfish reach less than 20 inches.

Puffers

Bandtail puffer *(Sphoeroides spengleri)* Two black tail bands terminate the series of black spots from the chin. This one-foot puffer and its relatives have prickles, not spines, on the body.

6 **Sharpnose puffer** *(Canthigaster rostrata)* A relatively long snout and bizarre blue markings identify this four-inch fish.

7 **Checkered puffer** *(Sphoeroides testudineus)* features a distinctive reticulate pattern. Length is about ten inches.

8 **Southern puffer** *(Sphoeroides nephelus)* grows to about one foot.

1 Leatherback
turtle

Sea turtles

Long-lived reptiles, sea turtles do not depend on land for any purpose other than to lay eggs. Though air breathing, they remain underwater for long periods of time. One loggerhead turtle in captivity was seen to surface for air about once every three hours. Front limbs have evolved into oarlike flippers. Sea turtles range over hundreds of miles in the tropical and subtropical waters they inhabit.

1 **Leatherback turtle** *(Dermochelys coriacea)* The leatherback usually reaches from 700-1600 pounds. Seven prominent ridges run the length of the tapered, leathery carapace. Edible, but sometimes poisonous, the leatherback has no commercial value except for the eggs.

2 **Kemp's ridley turtle** *(Lepidochelys kempi)* This is the smallest Atlantic sea turtle, reaching a maximum weight of under 100 pounds. The carapace is often as wide as it is long.

3 **Hawksbill turtle** *(Eretmochelys imbricata)* The translucent tortoiseshell of commerce is derived from the carapace of this sea turtle. Record size is 280 pounds, but 30-100 pounds is more usual. Hawksbill are set apart by the narrow, hooked beak formed by the upper jaw. This is another edible but sometimes poisonous turtle.

4 **Loggerhead turtle** *(Caretta caretta)* Reddish-brown coloration is the best clue to this turtle's identity, though many large sea turtles are so densely encrusted with barnacles that color is obscured. Largest size is about 500 pounds, with less than 300 pounds more usual. Though edible, the meat is said to be sinewy.

5 **Green turtle** *(Chelonia mydas)* Gelatinous green body fat gives this brown-hued turtle its name. General size range is 100-200 pounds, with a record catch of 850 pounds. Virtually nothing is wasted on this commercially valuable sea turtle. Products are green turtle soup, steaks, cosmetic oil and leather.

3 Hawksbill
turtle

2 Kemp's
ridley turtle

5 Green
turtle

4 Loggerhead
turtle

49

The coral reef is an association of ancient life forms that has been in existence about 200 million years. Its structure is dependent on individual coral polyps that range in size from a pinhead to one foot across. The slitlike mouth opening on each polyp is surrounded by tentacles that may sting and trap food. Limestone that builds reefs is produced by cells on the lower sides and bottom of the polyps. Living within reef corals are minute plant cells called zooxanthellae. These organisms are the primary source of color in reef coral, which varies locally. Each species has its own growth pattern, forming the colonies seen on these pages. Close-ups are provided where necessary for identification.

Staghorn, elkhorn and finger corals

2 Elkhorn coral

1 Staghorn coral

3 Fused staghorn coral

1 **Staghorn coral** *(Acropora cervicornis)* has individual branches up to one inch thick. Colonies may reach seven feet in height.

2 **Elkhorn coral** *(Acropora palmata)* is a master builder of shallow reefs. It has flattened, palmate branches. Colonies can grow six to ten feet high, and cover acres of reef.

3 **Fused staghorn coral** *(Acropora prolifera)* may be a variety of staghorn or elkhorn coral, and forms much smaller colonies.

4 **Club finger coral** *(Porites porites)* has blunt, swollen tips. All porites appear porous and have tiny, closely-spaced cups.

5 **Finger coral** *(Porites furcata)* tapers at the branch tips.

6 **Small finger coral** *(Porites divaricata)* has smaller branches than finger coral (above) and does not taper at the ends.

7 **Mustard hill coral** *(Porites astreoides)* may grow in bumpy mounds or pancake shapes and sometimes encrusts dead coral. Closely spaced cups set this apart from green cactus coral (below).

8 **Green cactus coral** *(Madracis decactis)* is a small encrusting coral with short knobs and visibly separated cups.

9 **Yellow pencil coral** *(Madracis mirabilis)* has more widely spaced cups than green cactus coral. Cups on both these corals have minute spines projecting from their edges. Yellow pencil coral has thin, blunt-tipped branches.

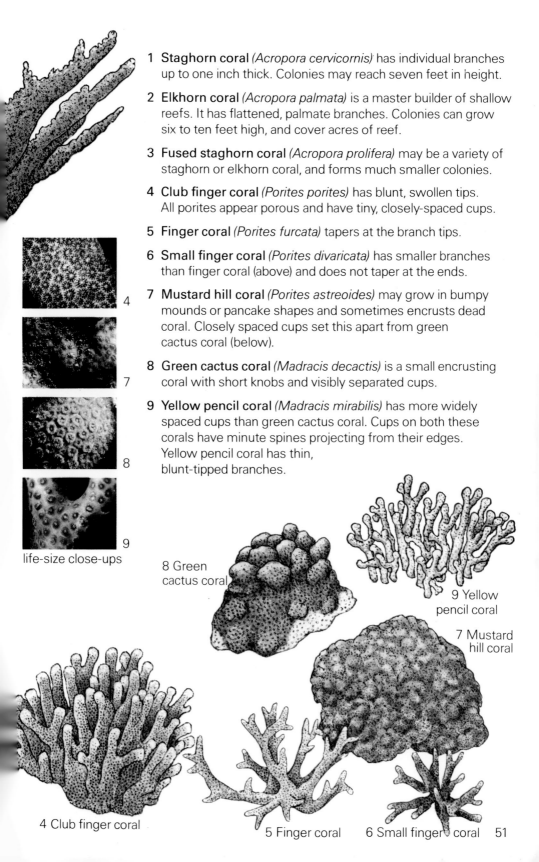

4

7

8

9

life-size close-ups

8 Green cactus coral

9 Yellow pencil coral

7 Mustard hill coral

4 Club finger coral

5 Finger coral

6 Small finger coral

51

Flower and star corals

1 **Mountainous star coral** *(Montastraea annularis)* is a major reef coral forming boulders five feet or more across and up to ten feet high. It is sometimes seen as thick plates or encrustations. Color may be green, brown or gray.

2 **Rough starlet coral** *(Siderastrea radians)* has deep, narrow cups that impart a rough surface to this under-one-foot-wide coral.

3 **Smooth starlet coral** *(Siderastrea siderea)* forms round masses over two feet wide with a smooth surface and larger cups than rough starlet coral.

4 **Flower coral** *(Eusmilia fastigiata)* has branches with oval cups at the ends.

1 Mountainous star coral

1 Mountainous star coral

3 Smooth starlet coral

2 Rough starlet coral

4 Flower coral

5 Solitary disk coral

6 Large flower coral

5 **Solitary disk corals** *(Scolymia lacera* and *S. cubensis)* are single polyps about two inches across.

6 **Large flower coral** *(Mussa angulosa)* has closely massed 1-1½ inch fleshy polyps.

7 **Elliptical star corals** *(Dichocoenia stokesii* and *D. stellaris)* have elongated, raised cups on rounded colonies up to one foot across.

8 **Blushing star coral** *(Stephanocoenia michelini)* "blushes" white when touched. Note the pale center in each cup.

9 **Golfball coral** *(Favia fragum)* may encrust on rocks or form golfball-size pebbles.

) **Cavernous star coral** *(Montastraea cavernosa)* has large projecting cups with ribbed sides. Boulders or plates may exceed five feet wide.

Lobed star coral *(Solenastrea hyades),* with its raised cups, has a "blistered" look. Height is about two feet.

Smooth star coral *(Solenastrea bournoni)* is somewhat like lobed star coral, but has smaller cups. It forms rounded domes rather than irregular lobed masses or crusts.

life-sized close-ups

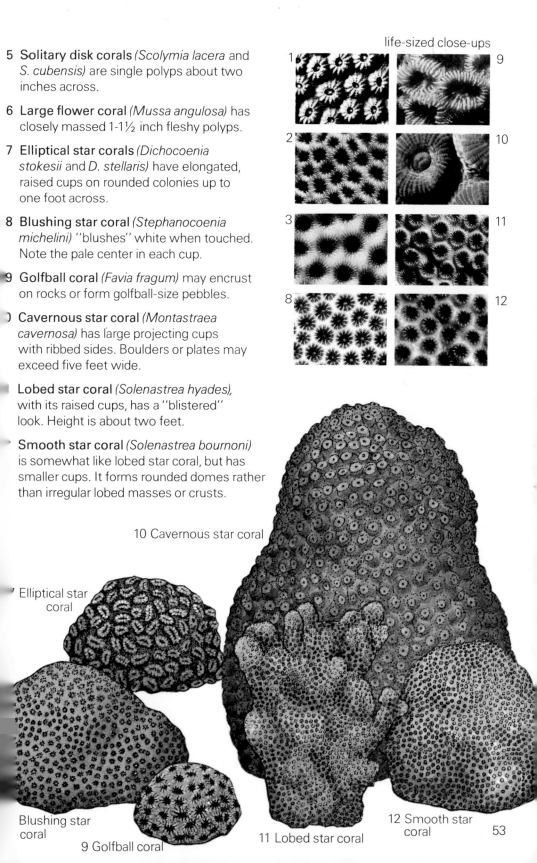

10 Cavernous star coral

Elliptical star coral

Blushing star coral

9 Golfball coral

11 Lobed star coral

12 Smooth star coral

53

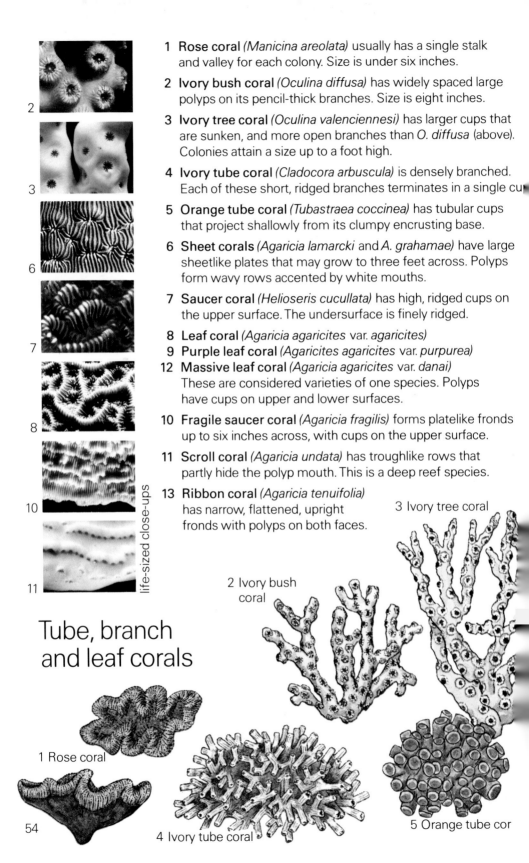

1 **Rose coral** *(Manicina areolata)* usually has a single stalk and valley for each colony. Size is under six inches.

2 **Ivory bush coral** *(Oculina diffusa)* has widely spaced large polyps on its pencil-thick branches. Size is eight inches.

3 **Ivory tree coral** *(Oculina valenciennesi)* has larger cups that are sunken, and more open branches than *O. diffusa* (above). Colonies attain a size up to a foot high.

4 **Ivory tube coral** *(Cladocora arbuscula)* is densely branched. Each of these short, ridged branches terminates in a single cup

5 **Orange tube coral** *(Tubastraea coccinea)* has tubular cups that project shallowly from its clumpy encrusting base.

6 **Sheet corals** *(Agaricia lamarcki* and *A. grahamae)* have large sheetlike plates that may grow to three feet across. Polyps form wavy rows accented by white mouths.

7 **Saucer coral** *(Helioseris cucullata)* has high, ridged cups on the upper surface. The undersurface is finely ridged.

8 **Leaf coral** *(Agaricia agaricites* var. *agaricites)*

9 **Purple leaf coral** *(Agaricites agaricites* var. *purpurea)*

12 **Massive leaf coral** *(Agaricia agaricites* var. *danai)*
These are considered varieties of one species. Polyps have cups on upper and lower surfaces.

10 **Fragile saucer coral** *(Agaricia fragilis)* forms platelike fronds up to six inches across, with cups on the upper surface.

11 **Scroll coral** *(Agaricia undata)* has troughlike rows that partly hide the polyp mouth. This is a deep reef species.

13 **Ribbon coral** *(Agaricia tenuifolia)* has narrow, flattened, upright fronds with polyps on both faces.

life-sized close-ups

Tube, branch and leaf corals

1 Rose coral

2 Ivory bush coral

3 Ivory tree coral

4 Ivory tube coral

5 Orange tube cor

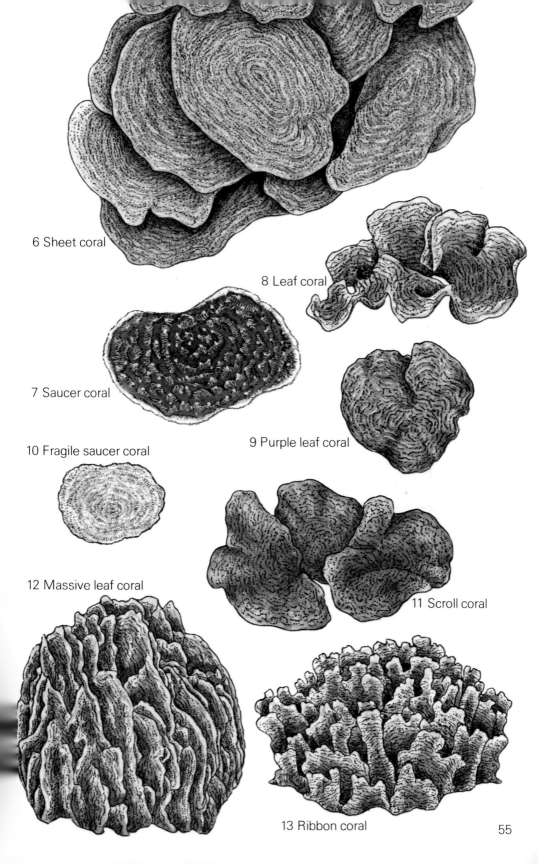

6 Sheet coral

8 Leaf coral

7 Saucer coral

9 Purple leaf coral

10 Fragile saucer coral

12 Massive leaf coral

11 Scroll coral

13 Ribbon coral

55

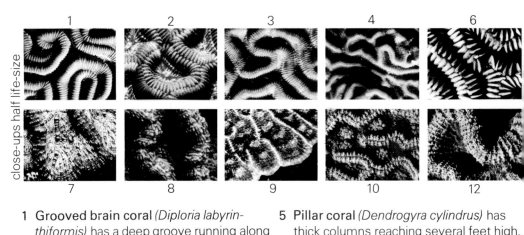

1 2 3 4 6

7 8 9 10 12

1 Grooved brain coral *(Diploria labyrinthiformis)* has a deep groove running along the center of its ridges. Size is three feet.

2 Giant brain coral *(Colpophyllia natans)* has a halfway break along the sides of its deep ridges, often associated with a color change from green to brown. Mounds reach six feet high. A similar species, *C. breviserialis,* has cell-like valleys.

3 Smooth brain coral *(Diploria strigosa)* forms regularly spaced patterns on domed colonies up to three feet wide.

4 Knobby brain coral *(Diploria clivosa)* forms flat mats or mounds up to three feet wide with an irregular, knobbed surface.

5 Pillar coral *(Dendrogyra cylindrus)* has thick columns reaching several feet high. Tentacles extend during daytime, giving a fuzzy appearance.

6 Butterprint brain coral *(Meandrina meandrites)* has ridges formed by thick interlocking platelets. Mounds may be two feet wide.

7 Fungus coral *(Mycetophyllia lamarckiana)* has ridges radiating from its center but absent from the center itself. Round or mushroom shaped heads reach one foot across.

8 Fat fungus coral *(Mycetophyllia danaan* has wider ridges and deeper valleys than fungus coral (above). Overall size of rounded shapes is up to one foot.

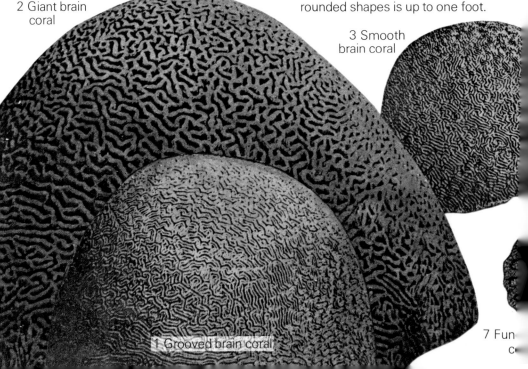

2 Giant brain coral

3 Smooth brain coral

1 Grooved brain coral

7 Fun c

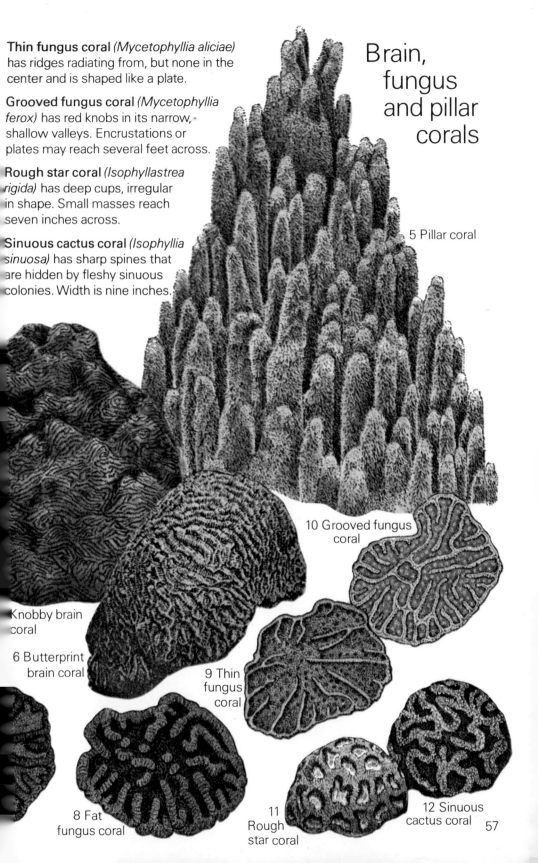

Thin fungus coral *(Mycetophyllia aliciae)* has ridges radiating from, but none in the center and is shaped like a plate.

Grooved fungus coral *(Mycetophyllia ferox)* has red knobs in its narrow, shallow valleys. Encrustations or plates may reach several feet across.

Rough star coral *(Isophyllastrea rigida)* has deep cups, irregular in shape. Small masses reach seven inches across.

Sinuous cactus coral *(Isophyllia sinuosa)* has sharp spines that are hidden by fleshy sinuous colonies. Width is nine inches.

Brain,
fungus
and pillar
corals

5 Pillar coral

10 Grooved fungus coral

Knobby brain coral

6 Butterprint brain coral

9 Thin fungus coral

8 Fat fungus coral

11 Rough star coral

12 Sinuous cactus coral

Gorgonians and crustacea

1 **Corky sea fingers** *(Briareum asbestinum)* have a flexible skeletal structure, as do all soft corals. Colonies may occur as lumpy masses or fingerlike rods rising from an encrusting mat. Extended polyps impart the soft, fuzzy look.

2 **Sea rod** *(Plexaura flexuosa)* has colonies usually oriented to a single plane. Polyps that extend from small shelflike projections do not alter the overall smooth appearance. Color varies from brown to purple.

3 **Spiny lobster** *(Panulirus argus)* has a hard exoskeleton that it must molt in order to grow. It is so delicious to eat that few live long enough to attain the maximum size of two feet long.

4 **Venus sea fan** *(Gorgonia flabellum)* faces water currents so that the greatest number of food organisms may be available to each polyp. Small side branches form at right angles to this fan, giving a more dimensional texture than that of the common sea fan. Color varies with locale. Height is two to three feet.

5 **Common sea fan** *(Gorgonia ventalina)* is similar to the Venus sea fan but has a flatter, more compressed surface. Colonies may reach to five feet tall.

6 **Deepwater gorgonian** *(Iciligorgia schrammi)* grows in water deeper than 50 feet. Color may be red or brown, with white polyps.

7 **Coral crab** *(Carpilius corallinus)* is a treat to eat as well as look at. Width of the carapace may reach to six inches.

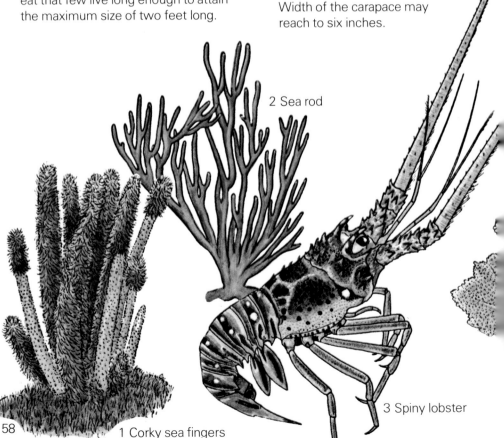

2 Sea rod

3 Spiny lobster

1 Corky sea fingers

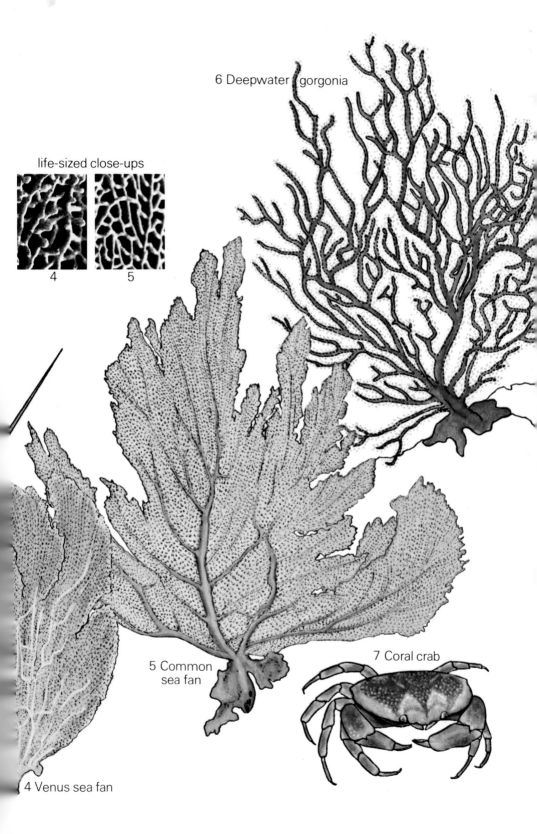

6 Deepwater gorgonia

life-sized close-ups

4   5

5 Common
  sea fan

7 Coral crab

4 Venus sea fan

Look, but don't touch!

1 **Portuguese man-of-war** *(Physalia physalis)* has scores of threadlike tentacles that dangle from its gas filled balloonlike float. Each tentacle has stinging cells capable of causing extreme pain, shock or even respiratory paralysis. If stung, remove all adhering material, taking care not to be stung again. Apply alcohol and consult a doctor. The float on a colony may exceed six inches, with tentacles trailing to 40 feet. The harmless, tiny man-of-war fish *(Nomeus gronovii)* swims freely with the man-of-war, enjoying protection from its enemies.

Jellyfish are not fish at all, but a more primitive organism. Rhythmic contractions propel jellyfish, though not strongly enough to offset heavy tides or wave action that may wash them ashore. All jellyfish have pendant tentacles with minute stinging organs that enable them to stun the small forms of life they feed on. These can cause pain on contact with skin. Avoid rubbing injured areas, as that may free stingers not yet activated. Alcohol splashed on affected areas is the best first aid. Failing that, a drying agent such as talcum powder, ashes, or even fine sand may be sprinkled on.

2 **Moon jellyfish** *(Aurelia aurita)* has a transparent, fleshy disk fringed with white tentacles. Size is over one foot.

3 **Stinging jellyfish** *(Dactylometra quinquecirrha)* is also called "common sea nettle." The milky disk may reach a diameter of over eight inches.

4 **Spotted scorpionfish** *(Scorpaena plumieri)* Among the dangers to man in the sea, most are of a passive nature. The spotted scorpionfish sits quietly on the sea floor, preying on small creatures that venture too near its well-camouflaged exterior. If touched or stepped on, wounds from its spines cause infection and great pain. If stung, consult a doctor. Size is up to 18 inches long.

5 **Red fire sponge** *(Tedania ignis)* may occur in a variety of shapes. When touched, it causes itching, swelling and pain. Treat with vinegar. Colonies grow to one foot.

All corals can inflict slow-healing wounds on skin, but none cause as much pain as stinging corals. Distant relatives of stony corals, they may vary in form from a flat encrusting growth to branching or leaflike structures. Polyps are very small and do not form visible cups, lending these corals a smoother looking surface than other corals.

6 **Square stinging coral** *(Millepora squarrosa)* has a boxlike appearance.

8 **Leafy stinging coral** *(Millepora complanata)* often grows facing wave direction

9 **Encrusting stinging coral** *(Millepora alcicornis)* forms branching colonies.

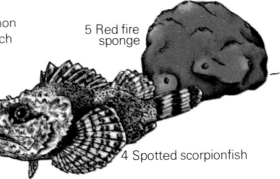

5 Red fire sponge

4 Spotted scorpionfish

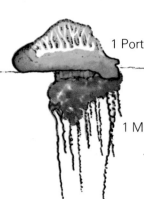

1 Portuguese man-of-war

1 Man-of-war fish

2 Moon jellyfish

3 Stinging jellyfish

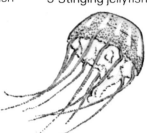

7 **Long-spined sea urchin** *(Diadema antillarum)* has a brittle shell, or test, with numerous movable spines projecting from it. If stepped on or handled, these barbed spines break off under the skin and become firmly embedded. Pain and swelling for several hours may follow. Remove as many fragments as possible and apply antiseptic or ammonia if stung. The test of a sea urchin may reach four inches wide, with spines up to 16 inches.

10 **Bristle worms** *(Hermodice carunculata* or *Eurythoe complanata)* The decorative white bristles on these worms are a form of armament. These brittle lengths of glasslike matter detach with ease on contact, producing severe pain for several hours. Sizes range from six to about ten inches. Color may be orange or green.

11 **Lesser electric ray** *(Narcine brasiliensis)* can deliver shocks ranging from a mild tingle to one strong enough to knock a man down. Electric organs are located near the sides of the disk. Maximum size is 18 inches across.

9 Encrusting stinging coral

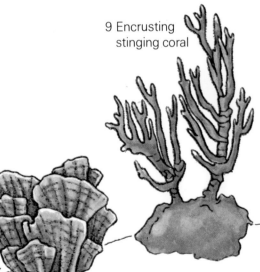

6 Square stinging coral

8 Leafy stinging coral

7 Long-spined sea urchin

10 Bristle worm

11 Lesser electric ray

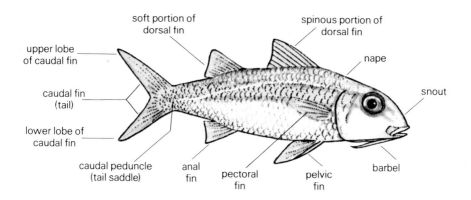

upper lobe of caudal fin · soft portion of dorsal fin · spinous portion of dorsal fin · nape · snout · caudal fin (tail) · lower lobe of caudal fin · caudal peduncle (tail saddle) · anal fin · pectoral fin · pelvic fin · barbel

Notes

Parts of fishes referred to in the text are shown in the diagram above. Size of scales where indicated in this book are approximate. Color phases illustrated are those most commonly seen, but many fishes are capable of exhibiting other patterns. Length given is generally the maximum size attained. Names follow those set down by the American Fisheries Society publication, "A List of Common and Scientific Names of Fishes from the United States and Canada."

Index